From College to Career

A Guide for Criminal Justice Majors

From College to Career

A Guide for Criminal Justice Majors

Barbara Peat

Indiana University South Bend

Boston   New York   San Francisco
Mexico City   Montreal   Toronto   London   Madrid   Munich   Paris
Hong Kong   Singapore   Tokyo   Cape Town   Sydney

Series Editor: Jennifer Jacobson
Editorial Assistant: Amy Holborow
Marketing Manager: Krista Groshong
Editorial-Production Administrator: Anna Socrates
Editorial Production Service: Chestnut Hill Enterprises, Inc.
Composition and Pre-Press Buyer: Linda Cox
Electronic Composition: Publishers' Design and Production Services, Inc.
Manufacturing Buyer: JoAnne Sweeney
Cover Administrator: Joel Gendron

For related titles and support materials, visit our online catalog at www.ablongman.com.

Between the time Website information is gathered and then published, it is not unusual for some sites to have closed. Also, the transcription of URLs can result in unintended typographical errors. The publisher would appreciate notification where these errors occur so that they may be corrected in subsequent editions.

Library of Congress Cataloging-in-Publication Data

Peat, Barbara.
    From college to career : a guide for criminal justice majors / Barbara Peat.
        p. cm.
    ISBN 0-205-33838-0
    1. Criminal justice, Administration of—Vocational guidance—United States
I. Title: Guide for criminal justice majors   II. Title.

HV9950.P44 2004
364'.023'73—dc22

                                                                    2003059520

Printed in the United States of America
10 9 8 7 6 5 4 3 2 1   08 07 06 05 04 03

Contents

6   Addressing Challenges   83

7   Politics, Politics, Politics!   93

8   The Importance of Networking   105

9   *Ethics*   *115*

10   *After Graduation: What Then?*   *125*

Appendix   *133*

PREFACE

Making the transition from the academic setting to employment in criminal justice or a related field can, at times, be an overwhelming process. It is during the academic process that students should be planning for their future careers, whether they start working immediately after graduating with an associate or bachelor degree or whether they use their undergraduate degree as a stepping stone to graduate education. Planning their future careers entails a great deal of thought. Future marketability, earning potential, and job security often rest on decisions that are made while a college student. The importance of careful, reflective planning cannot be overemphasized. Unfortunately, students are often ill-prepared to handle the task either through lack of personal initiative, lack of awareness, and/or lack of involvement with academic and career advisors.

The purpose of this book is to provide students who have decided to major in criminal justice or are considering such a major with information on how to best plan their future careers. The information presented in the chapters is designed to get the students thinking about their future and how they can use the time they have in college to better prepare. The activities included are intended to personalize the information for each student. Therefore, the book should be viewed as not only a guide but an interactive workbook as well. Completing the readings and sharing their thoughts with others in a class setting will give students an opportunity to use input and feedback from others to further enrich their educational experience.

Chapters 1 through 3 are tightly integrated in both concept and activities. The purpose of this section is to encourage students to reflect on their choice of major which, in turn, will assist them in their exploration of possible careers and the narrowing in focus on employment opportunities. Students will need to keep all of their completed work from Chapter 1 to assist them in their assignments in Chapters 2 and 3.

The information and activities in these first three chapters of the book can be viewed as steps in a process. For example, it is important to recognize personal interests, values, and strengths and weaknesses before making a decision on which career track in criminal justice to pursue. Chapter 1 is the first step. It is also important to learn more about specific occupations in order to make an educated and informed decision about future careers. Thus, Chapter 2 is the second step in the process. The information given and activities to be completed in Chapter 3 assist the student in choosing a career track, a process made much more efficient and effective based on the learning process of the first two chapters.

The rest of the readings presented in the book can be viewed less as steps in a process and more as integrated information which, taken as a whole, is intended to provide students with the development of knowledge and skills to better prepare them for their future careers. Chapter 4 provides students with pointers on how to make themselves marketable. Chapter 5 discusses the need to focus on the significance of developing skills in reading, writing, arithmetic, and research and their relevance to the profession. Chapter 6 addresses some of the general challenges to careers in criminal justice and how students can determine whether they are a good match or *fit* for the type of work they have planned. Chapter 7 discusses the importance of understanding the impact of politics on criminal justice careers from both a macro and micro perspective. This chapter also compares public and private sector career options, noting the general advantages and disadvantages of each. Chapter 8 focuses on the importance of networking as a college student and as a professional. Chapter 9 explores the meaning of ethics, the importance of professional standards, and the link of both to personal choice. Chapter 10 helps students integrate the concepts of the previous chapters and gives guidance for decisions about career changes, job promotions, and second careers.

The purpose of this book is to provide students with the tools necessary to make informed personal choices about their future employment in the criminal justice system or a related field. Considering the importance of a career decision, the student's investment in reading the material and completing the activities given in this guide can prove to be time well spent. Students will most likely find that what they gain from this experience is directly proportional to the time they devote to reflective thinking and activity completion.

The book is specifically addressed to the student reader. As such, it is written primarily in the second person. There are sections that are more general in nature and addressed to a broader audience. These sections introduce a concept after which the chapter gives more specific direction for the individual student.

Although the activities can be considered solitary in nature, the greatest benefit will come in sharing this information through class discussions. Instructors can use this book as a supplement to an introductory course in criminal justice, giving the students an opportunity to share their individual responses to the activities and gather feedback from other students as well as the instructor. Instructors can also use this book in a variety of classes to introduce students to a num-ber of concepts relevant to criminal justice such as the role politics plays in the criminal justice system, discussed in Chapter 7, the importance of networking, examined in Chapter 8, and the ethics scenarios provided in Chapter 9.

The book is designed to encourage personal reflection while, at the same time, recognizing that a great portion of learning comes from sharing ideas and gathering feedback from others. Therefore, students are encouraged to share their ideas in discussion groups and instructors are urged to encourage students to communicate openly.

Some of the examples and scenarios in the book use the pronoun *he* or *she*. This gender specific wording is used only to make the reading in these sections flow more smoothly and should not be interpreted, in any way, to imply that the circumstances addressed in the example or scenario are gender-specific.

Many of the chapters end with information related to the author's personal experiences in working with and for the criminal justice system for two decades. These personal accounts are provided to demonstrate the relevance of the information in the chapters to real-life experiences.

The valuable contributions made by the following reviewers are greatly appreciated: Stephen Brodt, Ball State University, and Bernard J. Dougherty, Western Carolina University.

1
The Heart of a Criminal Justice Professional

Much of what professionals in criminal justice do on a daily basis involves critical decisions that impact many lives. Very few other occupations have the amount of direct interaction with the public, oftentimes in stressful and dangerous situations, that criminal justice does. Added to this is the fact that these professionals have to continuously modify their actions based on the clientele whom they are serving and the situations in which they find themselves. The diversity of the population with whom they work, the variety of expectations, and the discretionary decision making of professionals in criminal justice make it a truly unique occupation. To take on such challenging responsibilities your heart has to be in the job, so to speak, because it is more than just a job. It is an occupation that impacts many lives on a daily basis. It is an occupation in which you have to be personally invested in order to give the public the best quality of service possible. It is an occupation in which you can make a difference. It is an occupation that has a life of its own.

Considering the challenges, it is vitally important, if you are interested in a career in criminal justice, that you educate yourself on more than just the job descriptions and expectations of being a criminal justice professional. You also need to come to terms with who you are as a person and how that fits the occupation you have chosen or are considering choosing. It is with these thoughts in mind that this chapter can be used to assist you in determining how your personal interests, values, strengths, and weaknesses match a career in criminal justice and how to find your best fit of career choice within the profession. It is important to keep in mind that personal interests, values, strengths, and weaknesses may, and often do, change with maturity and experience. For this reason, it will be more benefi-

cial if you view yourself and the occupations as continuously developing and changing.

Interests and Goals

Did you ever stop to think about *why* you have chosen or are considering a major in criminal justice? All too often students are drawn to a particular major for a variety of reasons that have little or nothing to do with any deep reflection on how their interests fit such a major. I have heard many different reasons given for choice of major, few of which indicate that the student has given serious thought to the decision. Some examples of these include:

I know I want to do something with people
It doesn't require much math because I know I'm not good at math
It doesn't require two years of foreign language courses
I heard the classes were fun
I heard the teachers were easy
There's no lab work required and that's good for me because I know I'm not good at the sciences
My friend said she was going to major in criminal justice and I want to take classes with my friend
The times the classes are usually offered fit my time schedule better than classes in some of the other majors I may have been interested in, and on, and on, and on . . .

Are these good reasons for choosing a major? Do these reasons justify the time and financial investment required? Do these reasons fit with the significance of the occupation? Most people would agree they do not. However, all too often students base decisions for their major on reasons such as these because no one has ever spent the time with them to help them look past such superficiality. Nor has anyone helped them develop the skill of reflection. As a result, they don't know how to reflect on their thoughts and feelings and develop their goals for their future based on such reflection.

You may have selected this major because you took a career choice test while in high school, or through the career placement office when you entered college, and the results have indicated that a career in criminal justice matches your responses. Although useful in providing general information for career direction, these tests often cannot or do not encourage the depth of reflection crucial to making decisions that will match your career goals with your personal interests, values, strengths, and weaknesses. Your preference for career may change dramatically between the time you took such a test in high school and the time you begin to focus on classes of your major, usually starting late in your sophomore or early in your junior year of college.

The first two years of the college experience can, and often do, provide students with learning opportunities in a wide variety of courses, broadening their horizons, and opening the doors to many career choices they may not have known existed. It is also during these years that students are maturing, gaining a variety of life experiences, developing new and diverse relationships, and frequently modifying, changing, or expanding their view of the future. It is during this time that they need to reflect on the reasons for their choice of major so that their future career choices best fit who they are as a person. Why? Because if there is a mismatch between goals, interests, values, strengths, and weaknesses, the student is most likely headed for poor job satisfaction and decreased job performance. This creates a situation that is of no benefit either to the employee, the employer, or the public served.

As a student, have you ever heard the question, "What sparks your interest?" When you are considering career choices, the basis for your decision had better be more than just a mere spark. It had better be a burning internal flame, one that settles into the very existence of who you are as a person—the heart of your interest.

In understanding interests as tied to goals, it is important that you be able to reflect on the general question, *Why did I decide to major in criminal justice?*, which addresses interests, and *What do I want to do with my degree?*, which addresses goals. Activities 1.1a

and 1.1b will assist you in developing answers to these questions.

Desires and Values

As a noun, *desire* is a strong wish, longing, or craving; as a verb, it means to hope or wish for, covet, or request. *Value*, as a noun, is something (as a principle or ideal) intrinsically valuable or desirable; as a verb, it means to rate in usefulness, importance, or general worth. Applying these words to our current topic suggests that, by exploring *why* a particular major was chosen, it is important for you to move beyond a simplistic or superficial answer, as exhibited through such phrases as "Looks exciting," "Seems like it would be a 'cool' job," and "My uncle works in policing and says it's great!," and move toward a more reflective, introspective application of the words *desire* and *value*.

To desire a career in criminal justice implies more than acting on a whim. It implies that you have thought through what you truly want, wish, or hope for. You are reminded to take heed of the old saying, "Be careful what you wish for, it may come true." Desiring or wishing for something implies that some thought has been given to what will happen if that desire is fulfilled. Selection of a career requires that you also think through whether your personal interests and goals match your desires and values and, in turn, whether your academic strengths also coincide with your choice of career. This whole cognitive process entails reflection and introspection and is what is so often missing when you are asked, "What do you want to be or do when you are done with your program of study?"

In exploring what you value it is important that you examine how these values fit with your interests and goals and, overall, how they fit with the duties and responsibilities of a career in criminal justice. Having a good fit between what you value in your job and what the job duties and responsibilities are as well as what the job has to offer you personally, can lead to high job satisfaction, better job performance, and lower turnover. Vice versa, if there is not a good match or fit, you may feel less satisfied because what you desire and value is not fulfilled through your employment experience. Consequently, job performance is likely to decrease and you are likely to change jobs because your *heart* is not in it. Activity 1.2 will assist you in clarifying your desires and values and will be used in a later chapter to determine your career choice.

The first three activities are designed to help you reflect on career choices. It is equally important that you identify personal strengths and weaknesses and reflect on how these may help or hinder your marketability as well as your job performance at a later date. Brutal honesty is an important feature of personal reflection and now, while you still have an opportunity to fill in some gaps, is the time for such reflection.

Strengths and Weaknesses

As important as it is to have a clear understanding of your goals, values, and interests, it is equally important for you to understand how your personal strengths may help you achieve your career goals, while recognizing how your personal weaknesses may inhibit your future career choices. In looking at strengths and weaknesses, I am specifically referring to knowledge, skills, and abilities that you may or may not possess, that are crucial to good job performance in most criminal justice careers, as well as required for continuing education in graduate programs. Recognizing your personal strengths and weaknesses in each of these areas while you are still a student allows you the opportunity to build on one while correcting the other in a user-friendly environment. It is important that you act on these opportunities before your job performance ratings, continued employment, possible salary increases, promotion opportunities, and graduate course requirements are impacted.

It would be a utopian world indeed if all of us possessed the knowledge and skills necessary to accomplish all job requirements and task assignments. For most of us, this is not reality. Even if you have a diverse education covering all aspects of criminal justice in particular, general education, and you are skilled at all kinds of communication, the ever-changing field of criminal justice requires continuous self-improvement and education. Understanding your strengths and weaknesses in learning and skill development will assist you in becoming a better employee in the future.

Just as determining why you majored in criminal justice requires reflection, determining your personal strengths and weaknesses requires critical self-analysis, being honest with yourself even if it hurts. It does you no good to continue to praise yourself for your strengths while overlooking your weaknesses. It's called denial and it will catch up with you sooner or later! Better it be sooner, when you are in a setting where you can still improve your knowledge, skills, and abilities, than when you are on the job. Activity 1.3 will help you begin this critical analysis.

Putting It All Together

After you have completed the activities at the end of the chapter, what do you do? You need to take a look at all this information together. Do your interests, leading to goals, fit well with your personal desires and values? Do your personal strengths in knowledge, skills, and abilities support your interests and values? Will your personal weaknesses inhibit your ability to pursue your goals? Do you have personal strengths that would not be used in careers you might choose based on your goals, desires, and interests? These are questions that need to be explored as part of your reflective process. Activity 1.4 is designed to help you reflect on your answers to these questions.

Think of your goals as a parachute under which all other areas discussed fall. Like a chute, if you increase the tension on one of the lines, the direction will be altered. Likewise, if the desires, values, and strengths/weaknesses change, the goal will also need modification. On the other hand, if the goal does not have enough support from your interests, values, and

FIGURE 1.1 Free Fall

strengths, it will start to collapse in on itself just as a chute will without enough air current.

You might think of the air current in this scenario as your motivation. Maintaining an even tension on the lines and being able to keep on track will require that the interests, values, and strengths support the goal and your motivation keeps the whole process in motion.

As time goes by and you gain experience, you may find that you want or need to change career course. Keep in mind that the word *change* does not mean 'fail.' It just means that direction has shifted. This is somewhat to be expected as people mature. Times change as do context. People change as do goals, interests, desires, values, strengths, and weaknesses. What feels right one day may not feel right the next. People mature, and, with maturity, often comes different life responsibilities. Change is natural and to be expected. What can damage a person's job performance and sat-

isfaction is unwillingness or inability to accept change. This unwillingness or inability to accept change can leave you feeling deflated (unmotivated), like you are in free fall and can't control the direction. This does not have to be the case. Flexibility is the key. If interests, desires, and strengths change independently or in unison, you will most likely have to rethink your goals. You have probably all heard that people, on average, change careers at least three times during their working years. It is almost an expected occurrence these days. Unfortunately, there are also some people forced to change their career, due to downsizing, medical restrictions, or relocation, who feel at a loss in figuring out how to start over. The process you just worked through in completing the activities is useful not just for those of you who are transitioning from an educational setting into a career. The exercises are also useful tools for redirecting your career. Remember, just because your direction changes does not necessarily mean that the direction will be a nosedive to self-destruction. Direction can change laterally and upward as well. Closing your eyes to change will most likely send you into free fall. Opening your eyes and regaining your insights and utilizing your skills will more than likely level you off and get you on a positive, self-fulfilling track once again.

The concepts and information presented in this chapter, as well as throughout the book, are not just ideas snatched from space. They come from years of trial and error: from running into brick walls, falling down, and starting over time and again. Instead of providing a chapter conclusion as a form of summary, examples will be used from the author's personal experience to illustrate the main points of some of the chapters.

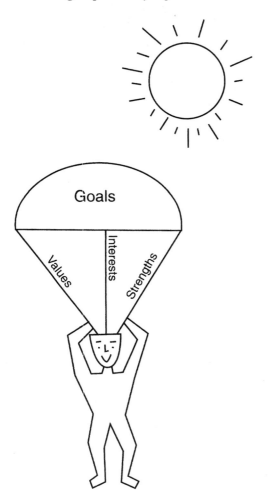

FIGURE 1.2   Back on Track and Sailing High

Personal Experience

I originally thought that I wanted to get a bachelor's degree in psychology. I had a fascination with trying to figure people out, myself included. I was subscribing to *Psychology Today* by my junior year in high school. I entered a large Midwestern university with a declared psychology major but withdrew midsemester, second term. I returned to my home town and enrolled in the local community college, undecided on a major. I took an introduction to criminal justice course and was captivated. By my second semester I had declared my major in law enforcement (this was the mid-1970s when two-year degrees with a practitioner focus were more common than the relatively new *criminal justice* bachelor degree). After receiving my associate's degree in law enforcement, I immediately transferred to a four-year college and began pursuing a bachelor's degree in criminal justice. During this period, many students pursuing a two-year criminal justice degree intended to go into law enforcement. I was no different.

I began a job in law enforcement immediately after receiving my BSCJ. After working approximately six months in this position, I determined that my goals, interests, desires, values, and strengths did not align; the tension strings of my chute were extremely unbalanced and I left criminal justice work. On reflection, I realized that I was inexperienced, easily influenced by media representations of what a career in policing would be, and lacking in skills and flexibility to make needed adjustments when my goals and reality did not coincide.

Fortunately, after taking a four-year leave from the field of criminal justice, I built up the courage to give it another try and took a job in corrections as a state probation and parole officer. I quickly found that I *fit* the position and the position *fit* me. My personal goals, interests, desires, values, and strengths aligned well with the position. I had many weaknesses but I was willing to recognize them and find ways to improve my skills to better meet the demands of the job. My tension strings were balanced, my chute was full, and I felt I was on a steady course to career satisfaction and success.

But, as I mentioned in the previous section, times change and people change. I saw many areas in the job where improvements in services to the clients could be made but I also came face-to-face with the frequently inflexible nature of a state bureaucracy. After six years in the corrections position, I felt a need for challenge. I wanted to try new initiatives, advance my knowledge through continued education, and have greater opportunities for professional growth and advancement. Once again, my personal goals changed and so did my desires and interests. However, this time, instead of removing myself from criminal justice work, I changed direction and was better educated on what that direction was to be.

You might ask, how could it be that at one moment everything seems to be aligned, heading in the right direction, working the "dream job" of a lifetime and the next moment you throw yourself into a form of organized chaos? As I stated earlier, times change and people change. It is how you manage change that makes a difference in where you eventually end up.

Managing the change requires the reflection we have discussed in this chapter. Completion of the activities will help you to determine your personal career direction. The next chapter will lead you through an exploration of ways to determine what career in criminal justice may be most appropriate for you. Keep in mind that you will need to continue to build on ideas presented in this chapter as well as information about yourself you have gained through completing the activities.

Activity 1.1a   Why Did I Choose to Major in Criminal Justice?

Check one or more of the following statements that you feel best answers this question for you, personally. If a choice is not listed, write in your response in the space provided at the end. Next, write a short essay reflecting on why you chose the statements you did. Remember, reflection is introspective in nature, requiring you to analyze your choices critically.

_____ I see problems with the criminal justice system as it is and want to be a part of the solution.

_____ I feel that offenders are treated unequally by the criminal justice system and I want to find ways to solve this problem.

_____ I feel that victims are treated unequally by the criminal justice system and I want to find ways to solve this problem.

_____ I feel that public protection should be the top priority in any criminal justice job and I want to assist in protecting the public.

_____ I want to work in a job that is highly respected by the general public.

_____ I want to work individually with people (person-to-person contact) for the majority of my time.

_____ I want to work to the benefit of people by networking with other agency representatives rather than direct contact with the public/clients every day.

_____ I want a job that fits well with my other interests and responsibilities including family, continuing education, and hobbies.

_____ _____

_____

Activity 1.1b   What Do I Want to Do with My Degree?

Check one or more of the following statements that you feel best answers this question for you, personally. If a choice is not listed, write in your response in the space provided at the end. Next, write a short essay reflecting on why you chose the statements you did. Remember, reflection is introspective in nature, requiring you to critically analyze your choices.

_____ I want a career serving the public in which I can be promoted into a supervisory level position within five years.

_____ I am using the criminal justice degree to prepare me for law school or other graduate program.

_____ I am intending to use the degree as a means to pursue a career in politics.

_____ I want a career that provides job security with good benefits.

_____ _____

_____

_____ _____

_____

_____ _____

_____

Activity 1.2   Desires and Values

From the list below, check your top five choices (check only five). After you have determined your top five choices, prioritize the choices 1 to 5, with 1 being the most important to you and 5 being the least important to you.

_____ Good wages

_____ Job security

_____ Good benefits

_____ Interesting work

_____ Positive relations with coworkers

_____ Working as part of a team

_____ Helping others

_____ Chance to benefit society or the community

_____ A feeling of accomplishment

_____ Autonomy or independence

_____ High prestige or status

_____ Special perks

_____ Ethical and honest work practices

_____ Freedom from stress

_____ Fun work environment

_____ Learning opportunities

_____ Opportunity for advancement

_____ Work/life balance

_____ Considerate and trustworthy supervisors

_____ Recognition

_____ Involvement in decision making

_____ Fair distribution of rewards

_____ A sense of pride in your organization

Activity 1.3   An Analysis of Strengths and Weaknesses

For each item in the following list put an "S" beside those that you feel are personal strengths you currently possess and a "W" beside the ones that you feel are personal weaknesses. Use the blanks at the end to write in any additional areas not covered. Write an essay providing the rationale (the *why*) for your responses. In explaining your weaknesses, also describe what actions you are going to take to overcome these deficits.

_____ short-term memory retention (forty-eight hours or less)

_____ long-term memory retention (retain information from one semester to the next)

_____ writing mechanics (punctuation, grammar, spelling, and sentence structure)

_____ essay writing (paragraph construction, use of transitions, organization, clarity)

_____ verbal communication skills (able to clearly state your point, argue and defend your position, ask questions)

_____ verbal presentation skills (speech in front of an audience)

_____ computer presentation skills (both for written reports as well as verbal presentations including ability to create tables and charts, spreadsheets, and PowerPoint presentations)

_____ reading comprehension (can read a report, a chapter, an article, etc., and clearly summarize main points)

_____ research methodology (design a study that explores a topic in criminal justice, select or develop an appropriate measurement instrument, gather data, analyze results, and draw conclusions)

_____ team work (share responsibilities and willingness to negotiate)

_____ time management (completes tasks before or on time in a consistent manner and balances time between personal, work, and academic responsibilities)

_____ punctuality (on time for meetings and other events at least 90 percent of the time)

_____ leadership (can organize tasks, motivate subordinates, and delegate authority)

_____ regular awareness of current events, locally as well as nationally and internationally, in a broad range of areas including political, social, criminal justice, and economics

_____ ethical/moral professional conduct (have a clear understanding of your own personal ethics and stand by them)

_____ multitasking and ability to prioritize (when given numerous assignments all due at about the same time you can organize your time and complete everything)

_____ _____

_____ _____

_____ _____

_____ _____

_____ _____

Activity 1.4   Putting It All Together

Go back over your responses to activities one through three. Write a reflective summary of what you have discovered about yourself through these activities. Be sure to pay particular attention to areas of consistency and inconsistency between your goals, interests, values, and strengths and weaknesses. Remember that it is better that you poke and prod at these issues now than after you have accepted a position and discover your heart is not in it. Also keep in mind that no one is judging you, there are no right or wrong answers, and what you take from this exercise is generally equal to what you put into it.

_____

_____

_____

_____

_____

_____

_____

_____

_____

_____

_____

_____

_____

_____

_____

_____

2
What to Expect: Looking at Career Tracks

As you learned from the activities of Chapter 1, important career decisions take critical self-analysis. To have this occur you need to take the time to reflect on *why* you have chosen criminal justice as your major, what you want to do with the degree, and how your interests and desires fit with your values, strengths, and weaknesses. The next step in making the transition from student to professional is to educate yourself not only on what types of jobs are available in criminal justice, but also the general expectations of work in these jobs. Knowledge in this area will only come from an active choice on your part to learn all you can about employment opportunities and job responsibilities. The information in this chapter is designed to assist you in gaining this knowledge as well as to help you with the decisions you will be making as you complete the activities in Chapter 3.

Career Tracks

When students come to me with what they usually consider an easy question: "What kind of job can I get with a major in criminal justice?" I respond with more questions. I start by asking if they have any particular desire, interest, or goal for a career in any one particular area such as in policing, courts, or corrections. If they already have a direction in mind, I ask whether they have a particular job in mind. If so, then I follow up with a question relevant to whether they are aware of the type of work involved in the job they have an interest in. Even if students have a reasonably solid idea of the type of job they want, I commonly find that they do not have a clear understanding of the job responsi-

bilities and the day-to-day involvement of someone who works in this particular occupation. What I see as an unfortunate consequence of the number of criminal justice-related television shows flooding prime-time viewing is the creation of a false sense of what a particular job in criminal justice entails. The way professions are portrayed by the media may or may not be closely aligned with reality. Just as we have the caveat in business, "Let the buyer beware," we need to also have a caveat, "Let the viewer beware." It will come as a surprise to almost no one that once you turn a camera on someone, as in reality-TV programs, behavior will be altered. It must also be kept in mind that, even if the television show supposedly depicts actual employees performing real services, the show usually only portrays a portion of that person's workday or week.

To gain a better understanding of the realities of a job you should utilize any one or more of the following strategies:

Research information about a career choice using Web connections, library books, textbooks, information at the local career placement office, and so on. (an abbreviated list of resources is included at the end of this chapter).

Use Web sites to find job descriptions that list job duties and responsibilities.

Interview someone who does the job you are interested in (an activity you can use for one of your assignments in Chapter 3).

Enroll in an internship program with an agency you are interested in finding out more about as well as being an intern with someone who holds the job you are considering (a subject that will receive more attention in Chapter 4).

Do volunteer work with the agency that has jobs you are considering.

As this list suggests, information gathering requires initiative on your part. It involves personal choice and, once again, reflection. It also takes time. In searching out the information, you should use your responses to the activities in Chapter 1 as a guide to the kind of career that fits your goals, interests, values, strengths, and weaknesses and match your responses to stated job responsibilities and duties.

In the following sections, information is presented relevant to the four main career track choices for criminal justice majors. This is by no means a comprehensive description of the jobs you might choose from, but it is provided to get you thinking and to help you narrow your focus so that you know where you may want to go for more information. The goal is to encourage you to again reflect on how all the pieces should fit together in order for you to make educated and responsible choices in career decisions. Activity 2.1 encourages you to use some commonly available career resources.

Postgraduate Education

If you are planning to enroll in a master's program, law school, or any other postgraduate degree program after receiving your bachelor's degree, more than likely you will need to start this process either at the end of your junior year or the very beginning of your senior year. Depending on what type of program you are interested in, you may be required to take some type of prequalifying examination, such as the GRE (general graduate programs), GMAT (business programs), LSAT (law school programs), or some other discipline-specific test. You may also be required to write an essay answering questions provided by the school to which you are applying as well as to submit three or more letters of recommendation.

You can explore your options for advanced education either on the Web or by seeking resources from your local university library, many of which subscribe to books that list all the schools in particular disciplines and the qualifying requirements. The choice of program will depend on your career interest. This is why it is so very important that you become focused in your career goals. General interest in management and administration of government organizations provides you with many more master's degree program options than does a specific interest in crime scene investiga-

tion or forensic psychology, for example. You may find that you will need to relocate in order to complete a master's program in your particular interest area. You may also find that a particular master's program requires you to be a full-time student with no, or limited, employment responsibilities. This can make it very difficult to pursue the degree of your choice due to financial constraints. I have seen students enroll in a master's program just for convenience's sake, for example, because it is close to home, the class times fit their work schedule, or the financial cost is within their budget. Although completion of such a program can still result in a positive experience, I have all too often met students that earn a master's degree in an area they have no interest in pursuing as a career. For these reasons, it is crucially important that you explore your options, plan ahead, and reflect on your future goals before making time and financial investments in an education you will not use.

What to expect   What you can expect will depend on many factors. For example, a single person with no children and financial solvency will have a very different experience in postgraduate education than, say, a person with three children who has to work full-time or at several part-time jobs just to make ends meet. The time that students in these very different personal situations will be able to devote to their studies will vary greatly. Likewise, students enrolled full-time will have a different experience than students enrolled part-time. General expectations of graduate school relative to undergraduate education will likely include some or all of the following:

> fewer credit hours for full-time enrollment (average of nine) than was required in their undergraduate program
>
> more writing and more reading
>
> more critical thinking and analysis
>
> more time investment in projects both at the university as well as in the community
>
> more essay exams and fewer objective tests
>
> more evening courses (however, this varies greatly, based on the program)
>
> more practicum requirements
>
> smaller class sizes
>
> more individual involvement with faculty
>
> more group projects

You are cautioned to keep in mind that what to expect will vary based on the specific program.

Law Enforcement

There are so many different types of careers you can pursue in the general area of law enforcement that it can become overwhelming to explore the options unless the student is interested in a specific area. When I am advising students on career options, I ask them which of four areas interests them (postgraduate education, law enforcement, courts, or corrections, not that breaking it down this way includes all the possibilities), just to get them thinking about their future direction. If they respond that they are most interested in law enforcement, I encourage them to identify their personal focus based on job responsibilities. For example, a student who is interested in being a patrol officer, whether it be for the city, county, or state, will want to learn about expectations in that career. These expectations will most likely be very different than those of a student who expresses an interest in crime scene investigation or forensic science, although both students are interested in a career in law enforcement.

If you are interested in being a law enforcement officer some things you will want to keep in mind include:

Patrol service is seven days a week, twenty-four hours a day, meaning that varied shift work is commonly a part of the job and days off may vary (this is not a Monday through Friday, 8–5 job).

New hires will most likely have to attend an academy for certification, which will require time away from home, sometimes several weeks in a location far from home.

Expenses may be incurred after being hired, such as purchasing a weapon, uniform, and so on.

There is a time lag between application and hiring while the department conducts its selection process, including, but not limited to, background investigations, polygraph, interviews, oral testing, physical examination, psychological evaluation, and a fitness test.

Length of time on probationary status varies by department but on average is about one year.

Promotion opportunities will vary based on size of the department.

Opportunities to specialize in specific areas such as bomb squad, narcotics investigations, detective bureau,

SWAT team, and so forth, will vary based on the size of the department and training and/or education requirements.

This list of factors to consider can also be used as a guide for questions to ask during an interview. It is important that you be aware not only of what to keep in mind when considering a career in law enforcement, but what can be some general expectations in this line of work.

What to expect

Overtime may be a requirement and not an option.

Day-to-day activities seldom are as exciting or intense as what is portrayed in the media.

Many federal law enforcement positions require relocation.

If your plan is to work as a sheriff's deputy, many departments still require new hires to work as a jail officer for a few years before moving into a patrol position.

If your plan is to become a detective, you will most likely need to work street patrol first.

You may be required to work swing shift, and opportunities for shift choice is often based on seniority.

Salaries will vary dramatically based on department; in general, starting salaries are in the low $20,000s to the mid to high $30,000s for city, county, and state officers and starting in the low $30,000s to the mid $40,000s for federal employees.

College education may be a requirement, but there may be no incentive for college credits or degrees and education may not be positively regarded by other officers.

Courts

Once again, there are many options available to students who want to work in the court system in some capacity. Some students aspire to legal careers and envision going to law school and passing the bar exam. This choice entails many of the decisions and expectations discussed in the previous section under pursuing a graduate degree, but being an attorney is not the only career students can choose if they are interested in working with the courts. Some of the other options include court recorder, court clerk, investigator for the prosecutor or public defender, and paralegal, to name but a few examples. The chosen court career will dictate the type of hours worked, how much and what type of education will be required, whether the position will be term or permanent, whether the position requires public election, whether travel will be required, and whether relocation will be necessary.

When students first come to me for advice about a job working with the courts I ask them what goals they have in mind. The majority of the students want to be attorneys. However, many times I sense a reluctance to complete all the graduate education required or a concern that their grade-point average or LSAT scores will prohibit their acceptance. In other instances, it is obvious that being an attorney has been a life-long dream and preparation has been made for the challenges ahead. These are the students who entered their undergraduate study with a plan established to put them in the best possible position to get into law school with a combination of coursework and good grades. These are also usually the students who have educated themselves about the requirements for law school and have planned accordingly.

However, for many other students, the appeal to be an attorney is not strongly grounded in adequate planning but is the result, yet again, of seeing the profession portrayed as glamorous in the media. If you are one of those students who is committed to the idea that this is a career you would like to pursue, I urge you, before you make the time and financial investment in law school, to educate yourself on what is going to be the personal, emotional, and financial cost of pursuing a career you may, in fact, know little about. How do you do this?

Complete an internship at a law office.

Job shadow an attorney in the type of law you are interested in.

Interview a variety of attorneys who hold positions you may wish to pursue.

Educate yourself on the variance in law school requirements and develop a list of schools to which you may want to apply with a corresponding list of requirements.

Learn about the job market for attorneys and make plans accordingly (information can be obtained in *Occupation Outlook*, usually located in the reference section of the college library).

Some of you may decide that you do, in fact, want to be a lawyer, while others of you may decide that, although you want to work with the courts, being an attorney is not for you. If you want to work with the courts in some capacity, but not as an attorney, I recommend that you educate yourself on the other jobs available. You can do this through contact with your academic advisor, the university career office, library materials, internships, volunteer work, interviews with current employees, and job shadowing, to name but a few of the possible sources.

What to expect   As mentioned earlier, job expectations will depend on the type of career in court work you choose. Some of the more general expectations can include:

many of these jobs will be Monday through Friday, daytime hours

politics can play a major role in job security

salary and benefits will vary based on government or contractual positions

locations for many court positions are in the county seat or metropolitan areas

Corrections

Corrections is a criminal justice field in which the options for employment are numerous and cover a broad range of educational requirements and work responsibilities, as well as salary ranges. Employment in this area may require some type of certification or academy training similar to what is required in law enforcement, primarily for correctional officer positions. Probation and parole work is another employment field in corrections. These positions are more likely to require some higher education credits, if not a degree, as well as training after hire. A position as a correctional officer or a probation or parole officer is more than likely going to be government employment. There are, however, numerous careers in corrections that can either be government or contract employment or provided through the private sector, for example, case manager, counselor, psychologist, classification officer, health-care professional, educator, vocational trainer, recreational facilitator, spiritual advisor, public relations officer, or legal consultant.

As in law enforcement, correctional services are provided twenty-four hours a day, seven days a week, throughout the year. Therefore, depending on the position one holds, shift work, rotating days off, and on-call duty may be part of the job requirements. Other positions in corrections will fall more in line with court services in that they are more likely to be Monday through Friday, 8–5. However, along with more traditional hours, after-hours services may be required, depending on the situation which, in correctional work, is quite often. For example, probation and parole officers are frequently required to respond to emergency situations with their clients during off-duty hours. The same situation can occur with counselors, psychologists, and most of the other positions already mentioned. Educational requirements will also vary, as will the salary.

It is your responsibility to educate yourself on the options. If you are interested in corrections as a career opportunity, how can you find out more about this career option?

Complete an internship in the position you are interested in.

Do volunteer work with an agency or institution to find out more about career options.

Interview someone who holds the position in which you are interested.

Use the university library and the career placement office.

Read descriptions of careers in this field, available in textbooks and other sources (a suggested list is included at the end of this chapter).

Attend career fairs and talk with representatives from the various agencies.

What to expect So what can you expect if you pursue a career in corrections? Although job responsibilities vary greatly, based on the position held, some general expectations include:

Some shift work may be required and off-duty hours will most likely be necessary.

Politics can have a major impact on job security.

Salary and benefits will vary, based on whether it is a government or contractual position.

Many corrections positions are located in the county seat (such as for probation or parole) or in the vicinity of a prison facility.

Contract work through private nonprofit organizations that service offenders is frequently available.

Caseloads are generally high.

Required documentation through case notes and reports occupies a great percentage of the work time.

Community corrections officers frequently have to attend court sessions.

Other Factors To Consider

There are a number of other things you need to be aware of when exploring a career in criminal justice. These points pertain to all four of the categories discussed in this chapter, to a greater or lesser extent, depending on whether it is graduate education, law enforcement, courts, or corrections.

Testing

Some form of testing will most likely be required for graduate school, but may also be required for some careers in criminal justice. For example, many law enforcement agencies utilize some type of test in their selection process. This may be a reading, writing, language (such as Spanish), or math exam or a content knowledge test on specific laws of the state or some other topic. Probation departments also frequently use a test focused on similar areas as either a prerequisite for hire or for continuation of employment during the probationary period. Some court positions may also require a similar format such as for paralegal work, court recording, or clerk's positions. You should clearly understand this process up front: determine whether a set score is required, if you will be allowed to take the test more than once, and whether passing the test is a prerequisite for hire or for continuation of employment.

Academy or Certification Requirements

Law enforcement and correctional employment (in particular, correctional officers) often require completion of some period of training, which usually entails a combination of bookwork and physical fitness training. Time spent in training varies, based on state regulations, but can be expected to be anywhere from two to twelve weeks long. Whether or not you are paid a portion of your annual salary during this time period depends on department policy. The location of the academy is often close to the state capitol and frequently requires a residential commitment throughout the time of the training.

Other occupations require certification, such as passing the bar in order to practice law. Completing the testing required for probation or parole officers may be a part of a certification process. Some specialty areas in law enforcement require certification, such as for some investigative positions. The process for this type of certification usually entails required training in the specialty area. A number of other occupations require licensure, such as substance abuse counseling and social work positions.

It is to your advantage to educate yourself on training, certification, and licensure requirements when planning your career. You may find that you will only be allowed to attend training after you have been hired by a particular agency, or you may find that you can complete certification or licensure demands while still a student.

Education

Educational requirements vary greatly, depending on the employment position. Some law enforcement and correctional careers do not require any college coursework, while psychologist and attorney positions require extensive graduate education. Throughout the past couple of decades the trend has been to require more college education and to base position assignment, salary, and promotion opportunities on completion of some college courses or a degree program.

It is important that you not only determine what the educational requirements are for positions in which you are interested, but that you also find out about any specific requirements for coursework. You may find that some positions, advertised as requiring a bachelor degree, will give preference to students who have completed a minor in some discipline other than criminal justice, such as psychology, business, foreign languages, or computers. Employers, when advertising position vacancies, often have specific needs that must be met and, if you know what the trend has been for those needs, you can better prepare yourself for the job market by taking the requisite classes.

Background Clearance

Many criminal justice job positions require some type of background clearance. This is an area that varies widely based on the position as well as the government agency. Some background checks are as simple as an employer calling the listed references and asking a few questions. Other checks entail months of investigation conducted by federal contract employees or federal agents who extensively check educational, financial, employment, and family backgrounds.

You are advised to educate yourself on the level of background check required for the position for which you have applied. In this way you can better understand the length of time to be taken between your application and acceptance or denial. All too often I have encountered students who thought they could apply for a federal law enforcement position and get an offer within a month. They consequently held off until a month before graduation to apply and were later dismayed that there was going to be a six- to eighteen-month delay in the hiring decision while the investigation was done.

In addition to the time element, it is also important that you know the extent of the background check in order to better prepare yourself for what may, at times, seem to be a relatively invasive process. Knowing that a stranger is talking to family members, school teachers, bank representatives, child-care providers, and a host of others connected in some way with your everyday life can be somewhat nerve-racking to many people. Your comfort level and self-confidence can be impacted by a lengthy background investigation. Knowing the extent of the check before applying for particular positions is an important factor to consider.

Physical Requirements

The physical requirements for employment in criminal justice depend on the job. Many law enforcement and correctional officer positions require some type of physical assessment. Other jobs, such as counselor, case manager, probation officer, and employment coordinator often do not. In applying for positions, you should educate yourself on any physical requirements and how the physical tests will be done. Although there are certain federal regulations that prohibit discriminating against someone based on physical challenges, it is also recognized that, based on the nature of the job, some positions do require a significantly higher level of physical fitness and agility.

Geographic Relocation

You should be aware that there are certain criminal justice jobs that will require relocation as a condition for hire. It is important that you know this up front and take it into consideration when making decisions. These positions tend to be more in federal government work than in local opportunities but occur with state positions as well, such as with work in the prisons.

You should also be cognizant of the fact that you may have to relocate in order to broaden your opportunities for employment. You will likely be extremely limited in choices if you are committed to staying in a rural area far away from any major metropolitan community. Focusing on one state limits your choices. Many employment opportunities in criminal justice require location close to the county seat or the state capitol. If you decide to stay local you must also realize that you are competing with every other qualified applicant with the same goal. The number of job vacancies, the opportunities in specialized career areas, and the amount of turnover within larger organizations all contribute to the likelihood that the possibilities for getting into a preferred job is much higher in urban than in rural areas. You should take some time to reflect on whether you are willing or able to move, based on a variety of factors including family and educational qualifications.

Age

Some jobs have age restrictions, both minimum and maximum, particularly those in law enforcement. Maximum age restrictions are most likely to be a problem for students who have sporadically attended college or who worked between high school and college. Planning how long it will take to complete the undergraduate degree and how long it will take to complete the application process is important when age becomes a factor for employment consideration. There are a number of employment opportunities that require not only an undergraduate degree but also three or more years of relevant, practical experience. Combining the time it takes to complete these two prerequisites to be considered for certain jobs, you should calculate whether you have time to do so before the age cutoff. You need to know this up front in order to be realistic in planning your future career.

Continuing Education Requirements

Once a person is employed, based on his or her educational and experience qualifications, does this mean he or she will not have to attend school in the future? Simply put, no. Many criminal justice occupations require continuing education, the extent varying greatly based on the job. Some of these requirements can be met through workshops and training provided by the agency at no additional cost to the employee. Other agencies have an annual hour requirement that the employee must complete and pay for. In some occupations, continued licensure or certification will depend on completion of continuing education, whereas in other occupations job promotions and advancement will be decided on hours completed.

It is important that you know about the educational requirements of the various positions that you are considering as well as how those hours are to be filled, such as through paid training or college courses. This information is another factor to be considered when making a career choice.

Personal Experience

I found my professional niche in correctional work. However, I did not take the time to educate myself in advance on the various factors to be taken into consideration with state employment as a probation and parole officer. First, I did not understand I would have to pass a state test and that the test would have to be taken in a large city with which I was both unfamiliar and miles from my home. I did not know how to prepare myself for the test and I did not ask. Secondly, after accepting the position, I discovered that a two-week training program was required for all new hires. The program was in a community far from my home with a residential requirement. Being a single parent with a young child, I had to quickly make arrangements for child care. Third, I was not aware until after being hired that there was a requirement for forty hours of additional training annually. Again, although the advantage was that the training was paid for and provided by the state, it was far from home and had a residential requirement. Fourth, I had not inquired about the agency's position on supporting continuing education, such as graduate school. I had taken the job knowing that I wanted to pursue a graduate degree in the near future. Last, I did not take the time to investigate the opportunities available for advancement. It was only after working in the job for a couple of years that I discovered that the opportunities for district or regional director were extremely limited.

I readily admit that this lack of knowledge was my own fault. I did not know the questions to ask at the time of the interview. I did not take the time to determine the agency's requirements ahead of time. I did not educate myself on what the position of the agency was on certain factors that were important to me, such as continued education and promotion opportunities. In retrospect, I know I would have accepted the position anyway, even if I had known ahead of time that I would not receive any special compensation in terms of time off to attend college or that supervisory positions became available infrequently. I needed a salaried position with good benefits and wanted to get into a job that used my degree. Although those were good reasons to accept a position, the requirements for training, along with the other issues, created some significant bumps in the road and finally culminated in my moving on.

It is better to approach any major decision in life with as much information as possible. I was fortunate that I was able to work through some of the challenges and, at the same time, thoroughly enjoy what I did for a living. Such a positive result may not always be the case. I have learned through the years that educated and informed decisions are a much better basis for accepting a position.

Activity 2.1   Exploring Resources

Select three of the following resources and review the material provided in each. Write a summary of what you learned from each of the three resources.

Opportunities in Law Enforcement and Criminal Justice Careers by Stinchcomb, J. A. McGraw-Hill, 1996.

Seeking Employment in Criminal Justice and Related Fields by Harr, J. S. Wadsworth, 1999.

Community-Based Corrections and Guide to Careers in Criminal Justice by McCarthy, B. R., et al. Wadsworth, 2001.

Management and Supervision in Law Enforcement and Guide to Careers in Criminal Justice by Bennett, W. W. et al. Wadsworth, 2001.

Law School Admission Council. The Official Guide to U.S. Law Schools. Newton, PA: 2000.

The College Blue Book. New York: Macmillan Reference USA, 2002.

Peterson's Annual Guides to Graduate Study. Princeton, NJ: Peterson's, 2000.

Occupational Outlook Handbook. Washington, DC: GPO, biennial.

America's Career InfoNet at http://www.acinet.org/acinet

The College Major's Handbook: The Actual Jobs, Earnings, and Trends for Graduates of 60 College Majors. Indianapolis, IN: JIST Works, 1999.

Career Planning in Criminal Justice by De Lucia, R., & Doyle, T. (3rd ed.). Anderson, 1998.

Inside Jobs: A Realistic Guide to Criminal Justice Careers for College Graduates by Henry, S. Sheffield, 1994.

Careers in Criminal Justice by Stephens, W. R.(2nd ed.). Allyn and Bacon, 2002.

100 Best Careers in Crime Fighting: Law Enforcement, Private Security, and Cyberspace Crime Detection by Lee, M. P., Lee, R. S., and Beam, C. Macmillan Reference USA, 1998.

Guide to Careers in Federal Law Enforcement: Profiles of 225 High-Powered Positions and Surefire Tactics for Getting Hired by Ackerman, T. Sage Creek Press, 1999.

Guide to Law Enforcement Careers by Hutton, D., and Mydlarz, A. Barron's Educational, 1997.

Paralegal: An Insider's Guide to One of the Fastest-Growing Careers by Bernardo, B. Peterson's, 1997.

Careers in Law by Munneke, G. VGM Career Horizons, 1997.

The Changing Career of the Correctional Officer: Policy Implications for the 21st Century by Josi, D., and Sechrest, D. Butterworth-Heinemann, 1998.

Career Paths: A Guide to Jobs in Criminal Justice by Armstrong, G. M., and Armstrong, S. C. Prentice-Hall, 1997.

3
Choosing a Career

Determining why you chose to major in criminal justice needs to be followed with deciding the area of criminal justice in which you want a career. In response to the question, "What do you want to do with your criminal justice degree?" the majority of students respond, "I'm not sure," even at the senior level. In order to get the most from your college education it is important that you decide during your junior year, if not before, what area in criminal justice you want to pursue. Planning ahead and deciding which area within the broader discipline of criminal justice you want to follow will help you plan your coursework as well as which electives you want to take. A focused education with careful course selection can increase your marketability.

At first glance, career choice may appear to be a simple decision and, with some people, it is. There are some students who can give a definitive answer when asked what they are going to do after graduation. As a faculty member, I have encountered this most often when a student comes from a family who has a history in a particular career area such as policing or law. Who better to know the ins and outs of a career in policing than the child of an officer? I have also experienced the other side of parentally influenced career choices, students who tell me with conviction that a particular career choice is something they will avoid with a passion because they have witnessed, first hand, the impact it has had on their families.

Regardless, for many students, the transition between the educational setting and actually deciding on a career can be an overwhelming task. Many variables contribute to this feeling of being overwhelmed. One factor that often weighs heavily on students is the fact that after graduation the common expectation is that they will now begin full-time employment and become a responsible adult in society or, as commonly put in student terms, the party is now over. I have seen this particularly with students who came straight to college after high school and have attended school full-time with either no job or a part-time filler job used to support their education. Students frequently express what others may term a fear of failure—that although now they have the education, they may not be able to cut it in the real world. In this transition stage, many students will also experience the same feeling they had at various stages in school from primary grades all the way through college: Will I be accepted? Students in all disciplines, not only criminal justice majors, experience such doubts. However, the career choices to be made by criminal justice majors may, in fact, weigh more heavily on the mind than some choices to be made in other disciplines because much of the work in criminal justice involves direct contact with the public, often in difficult situations. Therefore, the "Will I be accepted?" question applies to being accepted by colleagues as well as being able to work with the public.

The weight of these thoughts can cause anxiety, and even fear, which can, in turn, cause inaction by students. They put off the reflective thinking and decision making necessary for choices they need to make during their college education. Students need to realize that delaying a decision is of no benefit and will negatively affect their ability to get the job they want in the career they desire. As I discussed in Chapter 2, many of the employment opportunities in criminal justice can take a substantial amount of time between application and hiring. Students must face the reality that, in order for them to be in the best possible position to start their career shortly after graduation, they need to make career choices while still in school. Moving beyond the choice of major to the choice of career can be a daunting task, but if students take an active role in making these choices through reflection and informed decision making, they can purposefully look for the best possible *fit*.

Goals and Specific Criminal Justice Positions: Looking for the Best Fit

The activities in Chapter 1 were designed to assist you in identifying your goals, interests, and values as well as your personal strengths and weaknesses. These activities focused on a reflective thought process or, soul searching. The information in Chapter 2 was provided to educate you about the many criminal justice career possibilities as well as to provide an overview of some of the job responsibilities in these careers. In combination, the general job information gained as well as your own personal reflections should assist in the process of determining the best possible *fit* between you and your career.

You should not approach your decision for career choice with anxiety but with excitement. This is what you have been going to school for over the past several years. You have been making an enormous investment, both financially as well as in time, and you have had to face many sacrifices along the way. Although everyone approaches this transition with the hope that they will find the perfect *fit* in a job, finding that fit may not come immediately. It is important to recognize that it is not the end of the world if what you thought was going to be your dream job turns out not to be a good fit. However, it is also important to feel that, regardless of what happens, you did everything in your power to make educated choices in your transition from student to employee, that you have control over your own destiny.

Choosing a career is more than just looking for a job. All of us can probably find a job. In choosing a career, we are trying to locate meaningful, interesting, growth producing, enjoyable work. When I asked seniors what they really wanted from their future employment, the majority of them said they wanted work that they enjoyed going to each day.

How do people know they have found a good fit between who they are and their career choice? When I asked several criminal justice professionals this question, I received a variety of responses:

Most days I feel energized just going to work.

I have been able to grow professionally with the job.

I have been able to learn ways to improve my performance.

I have a sense of accomplishment.

I have a sense of feeling fulfilled and complete.

Finding the Best Fit

The activities in this chapter will help you narrow your career choices, tailor the choices to your abilities, and give direction for deciding what to do next: begin a job shortly after graduation or undertake an advanced degree program. These activities will help you identify your career interests. Completing the charts, tables, and writing assignments will require reflection. There are no right or wrong answers, just thoughtful or careful answers. What you gain from these activities will be equal to the amount of effort you put in. Where indicated, be sure to use your results from activities in previous chapters. Also, be sure to complete all tables and charts relevant to your chosen career area. Each area identified refers you to a list of possible employment opportunities. You may find that you want to complete the activities using more than one career choice. This can easily be done by going back to the first activity and starting over.

These activities are designed to assist you in reflecting on choices you have already made and, ultimately, provide focus and direction in your career decisions. You should not interpret the inclusion of the activities as forcing you to make a choice of career. They are merely provided to guide you in learning the process of making career choices. Once the process is learned, you can apply these skills to any career decision, whether it be in criminal justice or another discipline.

Activity 3.1 Making Decisions about Careers

Use the following charts and tables to determine your career interests. Be sure to complete all tables and charts relevant to your chosen career area. Each interest area refers you to a list of possible employment opportunities based on that focus. Everyone needs to complete Chart 5 and everyone needs to determine if any of the other employment opportunities listed in Table 4 are of interest.

After completing the charts and tables, refer to the essay instructions and complete all follow-up assignments.

Career Decision Tree

Choose one of the career tracks below by checking the appropriate box and following the directions for that choice.

CHOICES TO BE MADE

| Continuing ☐ Education | Law ☐ Enforcement | Courts ☐ | Corrections ☐ |

Go to Charts 1 and 5   Go to Charts 2 and 5   Go to Charts 3 and 5   Go to Charts 4 and 5

Chart 1

Check the track that applies to your intent and follow the flow chart, checking yes or no for each statement. Note the recommendations for yes or no responses.

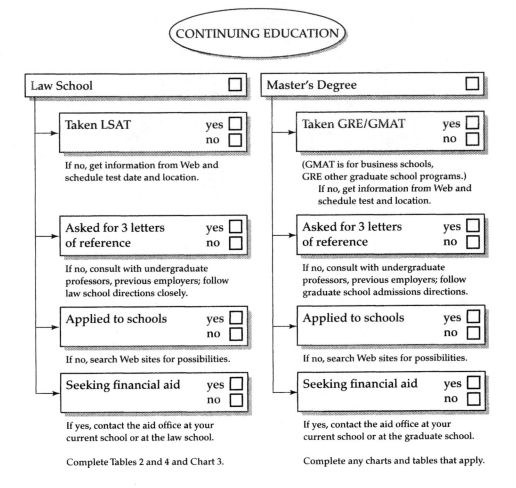

CONTINUING EDUCATION

Law School ☐	Master's Degree ☐
Taken LSAT yes ☐ no ☐	**Taken GRE/GMAT** yes ☐ no ☐
If no, get information from Web and schedule test date and location.	(GMAT is for business schools, GRE other graduate school programs.) If no, get information from Web and schedule test and location.
Asked for 3 letters of reference yes ☐ no ☐	**Asked for 3 letters of reference** yes ☐ no ☐
If no, consult with undergraduate professors, previous employers; follow law school directions closely.	If no, consult with undergraduate professors, previous employers; follow graduate school admissions directions.
Applied to schools yes ☐ no ☐	**Applied to schools** yes ☐ no ☐
If no, search Web sites for possibilities.	If no, search Web sites for possibilities.
Seeking financial aid yes ☐ no ☐	**Seeking financial aid** yes ☐ no ☐
If yes, contact the aid office at your current school or at the law school.	If yes, contact the aid office at your current school or at the graduate school.
Complete Tables 2 and 4 and Chart 3.	Complete any charts and tables that apply.

Chart 2

Check the track in law enforcement that applies to your interest and follow the flow chart, checking each box that applies. When done, complete Table 1.

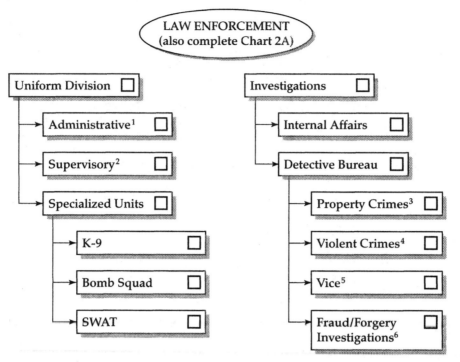

[1] Such as research and development, policy and procedure development, human resources, training
[2] Such as shift commander, sergeant or higher in rank, and so forth
[3] Such as burglary, motor vehicle theft, arson, and larceny
[4] Such as murder, rape, robbery, and assault
[5] Such as gambling, prostitution, and drug offenses
[6] Such as insurance, bank, home repairs, and so forth

Chart 2a

Check which level of law enforcement most interests you. Next, check the type of agency based on the level you chose.

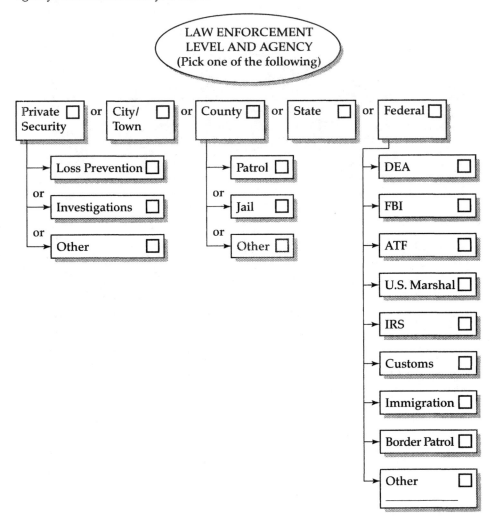

Chart 3

Check the track in courts that applies to your interest and follow the flow chart, checking each box that applies. Also complete Table 2.

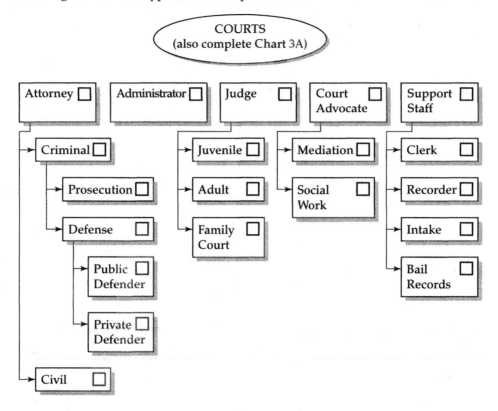

Chart 3A

Check which agency level most interests you.

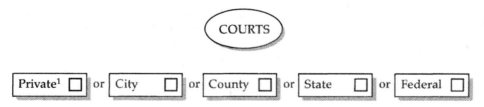

[1]Such as contracted services for legal, court administrator, investigator, and so on

Chart 4

Check the track in corrections that applies to your interests and follow the flow chart, checking each box that applies. When done, complete Table 3.

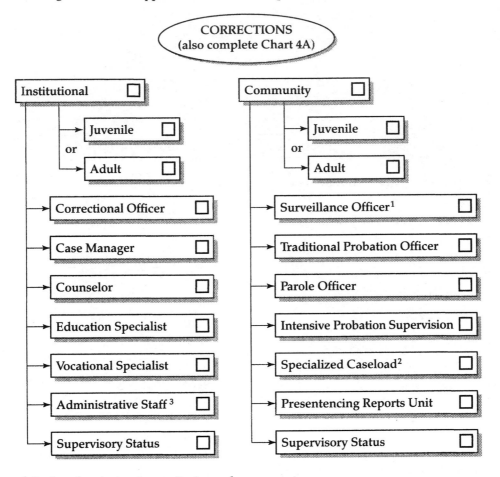

[1] Such as for electronic monitoring or home arrest
[2] Such as sex offenders, drug offenders, property offenders, and so on
[3] Such as policy and planning, personnel management, legal services coordinator, training coordinator and so on

Chart 4A

Check which agency of corrections most interests you. Next, check the level based on the agency you chose.

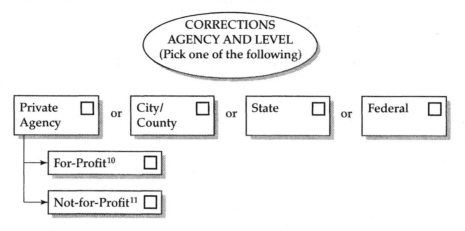

¹⁰ For-profit agencies usually work with private insurance companies to maintain operating budget

¹¹ Not-for-Profit agencies have government funding renewal through grant awards (called working from "soft money")

Chart 5
Personal Considerations in Selecting Career

Check all the following that apply. Take this information into consideration in writing your essay.

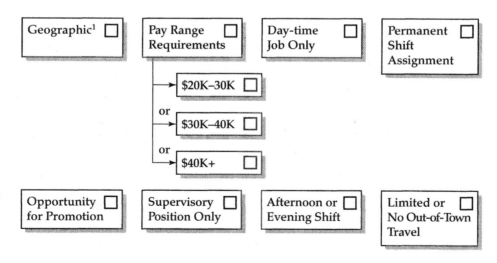

¹Do you have a specific city, county, or state in which you "have to" find a job?

Name: _____

Table 3.1 *Employment in Law Enforcement*

Check five of the following job titles that interest you. If you are interested in a job in law enforcement other than those that are on the list, use the space provided to fill in your choice. Next, rank-order your preferences with 1 being the type of job you are most interested in, 2 being your second choice, and so forth.

Check   **Rank(s)**

_____ Uniformed Officer[1]   _____   _____   _____

_____ Investigations   _____

_____ Traffic Officer   _____

_____ Sheriff or Chief   _____

_____ Highway Patrol Officer   _____

_____ Fish and/or Game Warden   _____

_____ Dispatcher   _____

_____ Community Relations Officer   _____

_____ Fire Marshal   _____

_____ Federal Special Agent[2]   _____   _____   _____

_____ Military Intelligence   _____

_____ Security Guard   _____

_____ Retail Loss Prevention   _____

_____ Private Investigator   _____

_____ Forensic Science   _____

_____ Crime Scene Investigator   _____

_____ Laboratory Technician   _____

_____ Other   _____   _____   _____   _____

_____

[1]Such as patrol, SWAT, K-9, and so on. (Use the space provided to list the position.)
[2]Such as FBI, DEA, ATF, Border Patrol, U.S. Marshal Service, Customs, IRS, CIA, Secret Service, and so on. (Use the space provided to list the position.)

Table 3.2 Employment in the Courts

Check five of the following job titles that interest you. If you are interested in a job in the courts other than those that are on the list, use the space provided to fill in your choice. Next, rank-order your preferences with 1 being the type of job you are most interested in, 2 being your second choice, and so forth.

Check   **Rank**

_____ Prosecuting Attorney   _____

_____ Public Defender   _____

_____ Private Defense Attorney   _____

_____ Paralegal/Legal Aid Counselor   _____

_____ Judge   _____

_____ Court Administrator   _____

_____ Court Clerk   _____

_____ Court Social Worker   _____

_____ Court Recorder   _____

_____ Intake Worker   _____

_____ Court Mediation   _____

_____ Victim/Witness Assistance   _____

_____ Child Support Division   _____

_____ Investigator for an Attorney   _____

_____ Other _____   _____

_____ Other _____   _____

_____ Other _____   _____

Table 3.3 *Employment in Corrections*

Check five of the following job titles that interest you. If you are interested in a job in corrections other than those that are on the list, use the space provided to fill in your choice. Next, rank-order your preferences with 1 being the type of job you are most interested in, 2 being your second choice, and so forth.

Check		Rank
_____	Jail Administrator	_____
_____	Warden/Superintendent	_____
_____	Correctional Officer	_____
_____	Classification Officer	_____
_____	Prison Industries Coordinator	_____
_____	Education Coordinator	_____
_____	Substance Abuse Counselor	_____
_____	Job Training	_____
_____	Psychologist	_____
_____	Parole Officer	_____
_____	Probation Officer	_____
_____	Social Worker	_____
_____	Case Manager	_____
_____	Legal Services	_____
_____	Day Reporting Officer	_____
_____	Electronic Monitoring Officer	_____
_____	Community Service Coordinator	_____
_____	Other _____	_____
_____	Other _____	_____
_____	Other _____	_____

Table 3.4   Other Employment Opportunities

Check any of the following job titles that interest you. If you are interested in a job other than those that are on the list, use the space provided to fill in your choice.

_____ Criminal Justice Research

_____ Criminal Justice Planning and Policy Development

_____ Criminal Justice Journalist

_____ Insurance Examiner

_____ Postal Inspector

_____ Public or Private School Compliance Officer

_____ Personal Security (Bodyguard)

_____ Home/Company Security Consultant

_____ Child Protective Services

_____ Income Support Division

_____ Airline/Airport Security

_____ Sky Marshal

_____ Other _____

_____ Other _____

_____ Other _____

Activity 3.2   Career Decisions: Essay

Write a summary essay detailing responses depicted in the preceding charts and tables, reflecting on the type of career that interests you as well as limitations or restrictions that might be barriers in this particular career. Include in your essay an analysis of your responses to the activities from Chapter 1 by applying this information to your career choice. For example, if you identified a weakness in writing skills, explain in your essay how this may be a challenge in your career choice. Remember, this is all about reflection. There are no right or wrong answers.

_____

_____

_____

_____

_____

_____

_____

_____

_____

_____

_____

_____

_____

_____

_____

_____

_____

_____

_____

_____

_____

_____

_____

_____

_____

Activity 3.3   Career Decisions: Job Announcements

Using your responses to the tables and charts, find five job announcements that relate to your job choices as well as to the restrictions you have indicated in Chart 5. Keep in mind that in Chapter 1 you had indicated your top five job choices. You may want to go back to review this information and make sure that it is accurate based on what you discovered from completing the tables and charts of this chapter. These five announcements can be in reference to one job or up to five different jobs.

Activity 3.4   Job Announcement Essay

Write an essay on what you discovered through your search for five job announcements. Be sure to reflect on what you discovered through this job search (i.e., whether you found it easier or harder than you thought it would be to do job searches, whether your restrictions may cause some difficulties in getting the job of your choice, whether the salaries are higher or lower than you thought they would be, any concern you have with the restrictions and requirements placed on certain jobs, and so on). Therefore, this essay should be a combination of reflective thought as well as detail concerning the search in and of itself.

_____

_____

_____

_____

_____

_____

_____

_____

_____

_____

_____

_____

_____

_____

_____

_____

_____

_____

_____

_____

_____

_____

_____

_____

Name: _____

Activity 3.5   Interview Questions

Develop a list of questions you want to ask someone who currently holds one of the jobs that you did a search on in the previous assignment. The list should contain a minimum of ten questions. Be sure to write them in the order and format you would use to interview someone about the job and indicate, in the space provided, the job for which you have developed your list of questions.

Job Title: _____

_____

_____

_____

_____

_____

_____

_____

_____

_____

_____

_____

_____

_____

_____

_____

_____

_____

_____

_____

_____

_____

_____

_____

_____

_____

_____

_____

Activity 3.6   Interview Results

Using the questions that you developed in Activity 3.5, interview one person who holds the position for which you developed your list of questions. Type a list of your questions and the interviewee's responses. Include the name of the person you interviewed, the position he or she holds, the agency for which he or she works, the length of time he or she has been in this position, and the starting and ending time of the interview.

Name: _____

Activity 3.7   Job Announcements and Interview Essay

Write a reflective essay describing what you learned through the process of locating job announcements and interviewing someone who currently holds a job that interests you. Be sure to include not only what you learned about the job but what you learned about yourself through this process. Conclude this essay by describing whether or not you are still considering this job as a possible career choice and why.

_____

_____

_____

_____

_____

_____

_____

_____

_____

_____

_____

_____

_____

_____

_____

_____

_____

_____

_____

_____

_____

_____

_____

_____

_____

_____

Activity 3.8   Task and Time Frame

This assignment requires that you develop a time frame for completing tasks necessary to put you in the position of continuing your education, obtaining one of your priority jobs, or both. To do so you must first develop a list of tasks that will need to be done, such as completing your college courses, writing your résumé, getting reference letters, taking government tests, taking graduate qualifying exams, such as the GRE, LSAT, or GMAT, conducting job searches, such as through the Internet, completing applications, taking government prequalifying examinations, such as for probation work, attending specific training to improve your marketability, and so forth. Next you need to project an anticipated completion date for each task. Development of this plan needs to be done using a spreadsheet or other computer graphics program.

Activity 3.9   Goals Essay

Write an essay describing where you see yourself (in what job or continuing education program):

a. One year from now

b. Three years from now

c. Five years from now

Write a separate paragraph for each of these time periods. Include the type of job or graduate program you see yourself in, the possibilities for growth in that position or using it as a basis for career opportunities with another agency, where you think you will be working (both agency name and the geographic location), and the salary you anticipate for each time period.

_____

_____

_____

_____

_____

_____

_____

_____

_____

_____

_____

_____

_____

_____

_____

_____

_____

_____

_____

_____

_____

_____

Activity 3.10   Wrap-Up Essay

Write a reflective essay describing what you learned through the process of completing these assignments. Be sure to include not only what you learned about the job but what you also learned about yourself during this process.

_____

_____

_____

_____

_____

_____

_____

_____

_____

_____

_____

_____

_____

_____

_____

_____

_____

_____

_____

_____

_____

_____

_____

_____

_____

4
Making Yourself Marketable

Now that you have a clearer understanding of possible career, it is time to get a clearer understanding of the job market and how to make yourself more *marketable*. The steps you take to improve your marketability are most beneficial before your final semester as an undergraduate. If that is not the case, however, there are still some things you can do as a graduating senior. The information and activities in this chapter are designed to help you understand what is meant when people refer to the *job market* as well as to assist you, personally, in determining how you can market yourself when you apply for graduate schools or employment opportunities.

This book is designed to walk you through the various steps in making the transition from college to career. You should read chapters and complete corresponding activities in the order they are given. Without the prerequisite information of Chapters 1 through 3, you will achieve limited benefit from the information in this chapter. Therefore, if you have not completed the previous chapters, you should do so before reading this chapter and completing the activities.

The Job Market

You may hear your professors refer to the job market, especially when they are discussing career opportunities in connection with content presented in class. You may also attend career fairs where recruiters refer to the job market. You may have family and friends encouraging you to major in a discipline that has an *open* job market. Whatever the context in which the term is used, you may not understand its importance if you are unaware of what it means.

Job market can refer to a variety of things. Most commonly it refers to the availability or unavailability of employment opportunities in a particular field, but this is a limited definition. It can also have a broader meaning as when people refer, in general, to the unemployment rate in the nation. If it is a good or open job market it usually means that there are many positions open from which job candidates can choose. If it is a limited or poor job market it usually means that there are numerous candidates vying for the same position, which will make it more difficult to become employed in the job of your choice.

The *job market*, therefore, is connected to a number of other factors including the economic, political, and social climate. Economic fluctuations can directly impact the job opportunities in criminal justice. Tax revenues are directly related to income and earnings. When times are good, with a healthy economic climate, more dollars come to the federal and state government for public service expenditures. When the economy is experiencing limited growth, unemployment rates increase, as do crime rates, which, in turn, precipitate the need for more criminal justice professionals.

A second factor that can greatly influence the job market is politics. Depending on the political agenda of those in power, there may be a greater emphasis placed on criminal justice issues. For example, during the 1960s President Johnson had a social service agenda. The job market opened for people interested in the social service aspects of criminal justice such as caseworkers, counselors, educators, and job trainers. In contrast, beginning in 1980, President Reagan strongly favored a crime control philosophy that emphasized being tougher on offenders and, in particular, drug dealers. This agenda focused on the law enforcement and punishment elements of the criminal justice system, and the job market opened for people interested in a career in law enforcement such as border patrol, drug enforcement, and investigations as well as correctional officer positions. Thus, it is important that you be aware of the current political climate of the nation and determine whether your career goals in criminal justice are aligned with the job market shaped by this climate. If so, you may find that you have your choice of openings available. If not, you will most likely find that it is more difficult to find employment opportunities in your particular interest area.

Social factors, in general, will also influence the job market for criminal justice majors. You must keep in mind that what is occurring in the larger society is frequently reflected in career opportunities. The criminal justice system functions, not in a bubble, but in the greater context of the nation, and even the world. During the 1960s the criminal justice system was heavily impacted by several events occurring in the nation, such as the civil rights movement, the growing drug culture, and the nation's engagement in military actions in Vietnam. Options for criminal justice professions expanded to incorporate these changes. For example, there was an increased need for substance abuse counselors within corrections. There was also a greater need for law enforcement personnel knowledgeable about the drug culture.

More recently, based on the terrorist attacks on September 11, 2001, the criminal justice system has made dramatic changes to accommodate specific needs for security and investigation. The focus on homeland defense brought about an emphasis on airport security, immigration and naturalization service investigations, and protection of the nation's borders. Although this identifies but a few of the changes in the criminal justice system based on the events of 9/11/01, it serves as an example of how events that affect all of society can greatly impact the job market in criminal justice.

In Chapter 2, suggestions were made for ways in which you can find out more about career opportunities. What you also need to understand is that the job market in criminal justice is constantly changing as a result of the impact of current events, not only in the United States but around the globe as well. In order for you to keep abreast of how best to market yourself, you need to comprehend the current focus in the job market. For example, historically, when the political agenda was to root out organized crime, there was a need for law enforcement personnel to be knowledgeable about money laundering and tax evasion. This required personnel who could understand bookkeeping and accounting. The focus on problems associated with illegal drug use created a need for law enforcement personnel educated about factors influencing the drug market. More recently, with the emergence of computer crimes, there began a need for law

enforcement investigators who understand computer language in order to investigate fraud, stalking, and hacking. The events of September 11, 2001 dramatically changed the knowledge and skills needed by law enforcement personnel, and a need developed for personnel knowledgeable about the organization of terrorist cells and skilled in a variety of areas including computers, customs investigations, and security assessment, to name but a few.

Criminal justice curriculums have had to change to accommodate these needs in order to better prepare graduates for the job market. However, the responsibility for awareness of the changing job market also rests with you. You are the one who will have to decide how your interests, values, strengths, and weaknesses fit with the ever-changing needs of the job market.

The information that follows provides direction for how you can better prepare yourself for employment marketability. If you are interested in continuing with graduate education, it is equally important for you to be knowledgeable about the job market. You can use this information in your selection of a major for your master's degree or an emphasis in your legal education.

While You Are a Student

There are a number of events and activities in which you should participate while you are pursuing your degree. You will be able to be involved in some of these whether you are a freshmen or senior, while others may only be offered as an opportunity during your junior or senior year, depending on university requirements or restrictions. In general, you need to keep in mind that you are, in fact, preparing yourself for the job market the day you become a student, not only through the courses you take but through the activities in which you participate. You should view all of these activities as résumé builders, a topic discussed later in this chapter.

Student Associations

Most colleges and universities have student associations with various agendas and emphasis on a variety of events. Some schools have their own criminal justice association and some belong to the national chapter of Lambda Alpha Epsilon, which represents students majoring in criminal justice. Students in these associations or chapters are often involved in a variety of events ranging from community service to academic conference participation to social activities and fund raisers. Through their involvement students have an opportunity to network with community agency representatives, develop their knowledge in specific interest areas, serve their community, travel to conferences and present papers, form friendships with fellow students, initiate extracurricular learning environments such as study groups, and become more involved in the day-to-day operations of their school. Students who participate in such events can demonstrate to future employers that they are willing to become involved in their education and their community outside of class times. This shows the employer that this is a person who is willing to go the extra mile.

The level of involvement of the association or chapter is dependent on the commitment of the students. I have seen some associations be very active in the community, academic, and social settings. I have also witnessed others that have floundered, meeting two or four times a year but never setting goals or participating in activities. Part of this will depend on the involvement of a dedicated faculty member who is willing to coordinate or, at the very least, advise students in their plans. If you are in a school with either no, or an inactive, criminal justice association, you can still become involved in a variety of events by joining some other club or association on campus. There are usually a number to choose from.

Conference Participation and/or Presentations

There are two main national criminal justice associations that you can join: the Academy of Criminal Justice Sciences and the American Society of Criminology. Both of these organizations have annual conferences in different locations across the United States each year. Both also have student chapters or divisions. You can take advantage of the multiple activities at these events to increase your marketability and to better prepare you for your future, whether it be graduate school or employment directly after completing your undergraduate degree.

You can independently submit an abstract of a paper you wish to present at the conference or you can submit a paper in conjunction with other students or with faculty. The paper is usually focused on a topic on which you have done some research. You may also participate in a poster presentation on a topic of your choice. Although a verbal presentation is not required for this format, it still gives you the opportunity to network with others interested in similar topics. It also gives you a way to focus your academic work on a spe-

cific area that can be continued in graduate school or through specialized employment opportunities.

Another excellent opportunity offered at these conferences is that there is usually an employment exchange. This gives you an opportunity to collect information from a variety of criminal justice agencies as well as to ask specific questions of representatives from the agencies. This, in turn, can assist you in gathering more detailed information than you can collect through Web links or reading material. Perhaps most importantly, you can practice your verbal communication skills if informal interviews are given on location while, at the same time, you can become more informed about the selection process.

Conference participation also allows you the chance to travel to places you may never have had the opportunity to visit. There are usually general sightseeing tour options available during the days of the conference so that participants can learn more about the historical, cultural, and landmark features of the conference location. There are also usually criminal justice-related tours whereby participants can tour prisons, jails, crime labs, and any number of other specialized sites that may be of interest. Traveling to various locations can also broaden your awareness of relocation options for the future.

There are also conferences sponsored by regional associations that are part of the larger Academy of Criminal Justice Sciences. This affords you yet another opportunity to present papers and network with other students and academics with similar interests.

Campus Events

Many schools will host a variety of extracurricular events throughout the year. For example, with advancements in technology there has been an increase in the opportunity for video conferences on a variety of topics, but the content of these conferences varies greatly. For example, the National Institute of Corrections publicizes the availability of this information to all members as well as possible interested parties; at that point a host location needs to be recruited. The host location is often a local college or university because it has the technology required. The fact that these conferences are often at the schools allows you the opportunity to extend your learning experiences beyond the classroom setting as well as giving you the chance to network with community agency representatives in a variety of fields. For these reasons, it is recommended that you take the time to participate in these events. They are usually free to students and last two to three hours. Attendance may also be required as part of a course assignment.

A school may also host symposiums or workshops focused on a variety of topics that students and community representatives can attend. Again, these events give you an opportunity to learn more about specific topics as well as allowing you a chance to network with representatives from community organizations. Attendance at such events can be included on your résumé, showing future employers that you took advantage of opportunities to learn more in specialized areas.

Career Fairs

Schools may hold an annual career fair, often directed at numerous majors, as a function of the campus career placement office. Divisions or departments may host their own job fair directed specifically at criminal justice majors. In either case, these events afford you an excellent opportunity to gather information and meet agency representatives. It also gives you the chance to practice your verbal communication skills, ask more specific questions about career options, and get an idea of the job market. You may also be afforded the opportunity to distribute your résumé and/or meet individually with recruiters for an informal interview.

Career fairs have another advantage. You save time because you can meet with numerous agencies in a single day rather than through individual contacts. You may be surprised at the number of options available if you just take the time to attend these events. Attending a university-wide career fair can provide you with ideas about job options in related fields that you may never have considered. For example, public school systems frequently employ criminal justice majors for specialized tasks such as security and counselors. Once you have a better grasp of the options available, you will be able to tailor your coursework and extracurricular participation to better prepare for the career of your choice.

Internships/Field Experience

Taking advantage of internships, or field experience, is an excellent way for you to get a better understanding of what is entailed in a particular job as well as affording you the opportunity to network with possible future employers. Internship involvement is also an excellent résumé builder. You can learn only so much from reading about a job and interviewing others who are employed in a particular career. The internship placement provides an opportunity to not only find out more about the inner workings of a job but also gives you a chance to determine if certain jobs would be a good fit.

Internship placements also give you an opportunity to network with others in a similar profession, not just at the agency in which you are completing your hours but also with other agencies in the same field. For example, an internship as an adult probation officer can afford you an opportunity to gain a better understanding of probation work while, at the same time, giving you the chance to work with other professionals in the courts and law enforcement as well as the city and county jails. All these contacts may prove beneficial in the future when you are seeking employment.

Internship placements are also an excellent résumé builder. Many job announcements state that prior experience in particular areas is required. Although often not a paid position, some employers will accept internship hours as previous experience. Whether this is the case or not, being able to include internship hours on a résumé shows that you have gone above and beyond the traditional classroom setting to learn more, and in a different context. It is important that you fulfill all your obligations through your internship placement and that you receive a good review. This can give you an opportunity to request letters of reference from your placement supervisors.

Commonly, students select their internship placement with the assistance of an advisor and can earn credits just like any other coursework. They may also be required to submit journals or essays in connection with their experiences. Internship placements are probably most beneficial during the junior or senior years because this is when most students should have some idea of what type of career field they would like to pursue. Students should be forewarned that there are generally very few paid internship placements. This can be difficult for students who are already employed part- or full-time. However, the benefits to be gained are multiple and it is highly recommended that, if offered, students take advantage of this opportunity.

Volunteer Work

You can also benefit personally as well as professionally from volunteer work. This is another opportunity to learn more about jobs while giving you the chance to make contacts with possible future employers. Many social service agencies are frequently seeking volunteers such as domestic violence shelters, child advocacy services, legal assistance centers, specialized jail programs, and homeless shelters, to name but a few. Volunteer work can run the gamut from assisting with phone calls to facilitating a prerelease program at the local jail or being a member of the sheriff's posse. The opportunities are virtually endless, but it is often up to you to take the initiative to find a place where you can work as a volunteer. You can usually find out about your options from faculty, your involvement with student organizations, and/or from guest speakers.

Volunteer work may not only prove to be a personally fulfilling experience but can also lead to employment opportunities. It is yet another way you can improve your marketability by showing future employers that you are involved outside the classroom in continued learning and service. You may also be able to ask your supervisors at these volunteer placements for letters of reference.

The time commitment is usually dependent on an agreement reached between the student and the agency. Because volunteer work is not commonly tied to college credit, there are usually fewer hours required during any given semester and no assignments to complete. Therefore, students trying to juggle part- or full-time employment and their other coursework may find volunteer work a more workable way of getting agency experience than an internship.

Community Practicum

Colleges and universities may also offer a community practicum for credit. Although some schools may call internships or field experience available for credit practicums, other schools consider a practicum to be a combination of volunteer work and an internship, with more of an emphasis on personal reflection. The hours of service per credit hour may be fewer than an internship but requirements for written reflections in the form of journals and essays may require a lot of time and contact with the practicum director can be frequent. The benefits already noted in the previous two sections, however, are the same. You will have to determine what opportunities are available at your school.

Now that you are more aware of the options available that can better prepare you for your future in graduate education or employment, we will turn our attention to how to market yourself once your employment search has begun.

The Job Search

The activities completed in Chapter 3 should have assisted you in gaining a clearer understanding of what is required in the job search process. In general, there are several factors you need to keep in mind when you are searching for a job in your preferred career area.

Time Investment

Just searching for a job takes time. You should develop a list of resources you can use to determine what jobs are available in your interest area, including Web sites, newspapers, trade journals (such as *Police Chief* and *Corrections Today*), government bulletins and newsletters, the university placement office, city, county, and state personnel offices, and faculty advisors. After developing this list you will need to determine whether you can use the Web to gather more information or whether you will have to make telephone calls, write letters, or conduct face-to-face visits. This first step in the search can be time-consuming.

The next step, which also requires a considerable time investment, is the actual first contact with the agencies. You may need to make phone calls to determine the application process, mail an initial letter of inquiry, go to the location to complete the application, or meet with a personnel representative. The important thing for you to keep in mind is that, on almost all occasions, this is a time-consuming process. You would be well advised to establish a time line to complete the steps necessary for the search process similar to the exercise you completed in Chapter 3.

There is often a time investment required once you have entered the selection process with an agency. It is at this stage that the employer commonly uses a variety of screening methods to narrow the pool of candidates. These can include psychological evaluations, physical agility tests, paper-and-pencil examinations, polygraph tests, oral examinations, background investigations, and interviews, to name but a few. For many criminal justice positions there can be an extended time lapse between one stage and the next in the screening process, and there are occasions when it takes over a year to complete this entire process. You need to be aware of the extent of the screening process and the time frame for completion in order to plan when you start your search and when you plan to begin full-time employment.

If you are considering graduate education, you also need to be aware that there are steps in the application process that require extended periods of time. For example, many schools require a qualifying examination with a cutoff score for acceptance. You will need to prepare for the test and determine test dates. You may find that you want to take the test over to try to raise your scores. This takes time, as does the actual application process, which can include completing required essays, submitting letters of recommendation, and visiting campuses to meet with review committees.

Qualifications

In any job search, you need to know the qualifications required for the position in which you are interested. How can you determine this? Through participation in the activities discussed in this chapter as well as your completion of the exercises in Chapter 3, you will be gathering information about qualifications through job descriptions, the application process, and personal contact with agency representatives. In applying for any job you need to determine first whether you meet the qualification requirements. For example, a position announcement for probation officer may state that a bachelor's degree in criminal justice, sociology, psychology, or a related social service field is required. If you are not due to graduate for another year, then it is highly unlikely that your application would even be considered. However, if the announcement states that either a bachelor's degree in criminal justice, sociology, psychology or other related social service field is preferred but a combination of college course credit and relevant work experience may be considered, you may be more likely to be considered for the job if you have some relevant work experience, even if only through internship placements. The important point to be made is that you need to read carefully the qualifications required and, if they are not listed, do some investigative work of your own to determine the agency's qualification requirements, such as calling the agency's personnel office and asking for the information, talking to someone who currently works at the agency in a similar position, contacting your career placement office for information about the position, or talking with your faculty advisor.

The importance of finding out about the qualification requirements cannot be overemphasized. It is a waste of your time as well as that of the reviewers if you are applying for a job that looks good without considering whether you have the required qualifications. This is not the way to present yourself as a professional

to an agency where you may, at some point in the future, be making an application.

Another job search tip: if you find that many of the job descriptions require a particular skill, it is important to stress your strength in this area. On the other hand, if you lack the skill, then it should be a signal to you that you need to find a way to learn the skill before graduation. For example, ads for positions now emphasize computer skills, and some ads state the type of computer program knowledge required. The completion of the activities in this book during your beginning years in college should give you ample time to improve your strengths and compensate for your weaknesses in order to make yourself as marketable as possible.

When applying for graduate school, you also need to know the required qualifications. Some schools have set cutoff scores for required qualifying tests, and this requirement may be combined with grade-point average. You need to know the qualifications required for the schools to which you intend to apply and make sure that your qualifications match the requirements.

Résumé

You can usually get detailed information about how to develop a résumé from your school's career placement office, and I recommend that you acquaint yourself with these services. There are also numerous books available that provide step-by-step instructions as well as sample résumés.

The term *résumé builder* has been mentioned a number of times in this chapter. A *résumé builder* is an event, activity, course, workshop, internship, volunteer service, practicum experience, and so forth in which you participated or completed that can be included in your résumé that will strengthen your qualifications for a particular employment position. Résumés are generally broken into six categories of information: job objective, education, experience, skills, extracurricular activities, and references (names and addresses). The categories and information depend on the format you choose. Whatever the format, the important point to keep in mind is that the résumé information should match the job for which you are applying. Therefore, it is possible that you may need more than one résumé you can use to send to different employers. For example, in applying for a federal position in law enforcement that requires computer skills and fluency in Spanish, you would structure the résumé to stress your fluency in Spanish.

In general, résumés should be relatively short (one to two pages) and use an outline format with categorical headings in the left margin. You should have some other qualified person proof read the résumé for presentation. Always check for spelling, grammar, and punctuation errors. Never cross off information on a résumé and insert corrections by hand. Make sure that the job objective listed matches the position advertised. Always ask consent from references before putting their names and contact information on a résumé, and make certain that the references you list can speak to your qualifications for the position. Be sure to update your résumé based on continued education and experience.

Cover Letter

You need to include a cover letter with your résumé. Example cover letters can usually be found in materials available through the university career placement office or in books specific to employment searches. This letter should be written specifically for the job for which you are applying and contain a brief introduction stating your qualifications. One big mistake that many people make is to write a form letter that is general enough to be applicable to almost any job announcement. What this says to employment screeners is: (1) the person is applying for other, and possibly many, jobs, and (2) the person is not invested enough in a specific job to take the time to write an individualized letter. I know that when I was an employment screener for professional positions, this was one of the things that automatically eliminated or limited a person's possibilities for employment.

Once again, you need to make certain that the letter is well written, without grammar, punctuation, or spelling errors. The letter should be addressed to the specific person or department listed in the job announcement, and the date on the letter should reflect the date of application. This is usually another clue to screeners that a form letter is being used, especially if the date on the letter is days or even weeks before the position was announced. The cover letter is usually the very first opportunity to present oneself and a poorly structured cover letter can automatically eliminate you from consideration.

The following activities are designed to assist you in applying the information contained in this chapter to various skill development areas while, at the same time, encouraging you to reflect on ways you can increase your marketability. How prepared you are to enter the job market will be directly proportionate to the time you have invested in the activities suggested in this chapter.

Activity 4.1a   Exploring Membership Options in Professional Organizations

Using the Web, locate information about the Academy of Criminal Justice Sciences (ACJS).

How much are the annual dues for student membership?

_____

When and where is the next annual conference?

_____

What is the theme of the next annual conference?

_____

What is the fee for student attendance?

_____

Of the different tracks or sections, which three interest you the most?

   1. _____

   2. _____

   3. _____

Activity 4.1b   Exploring Membership Options in Professional Organizations

Using the Web, locate information about the American Society of Criminology (ASC).

How much are the annual dues for student membership?

_____

When and where is the next annual conference?

_____

What is the theme of the next annual conference?

_____

What is the fee for student attendance?

_____

Of the different tracks or sections, which three interest you the most?

1. _____

2. _____

3. _____

Activity 4.2 Conference Paper Abstract

Write a 100-word abstract for one of the conference tracks or sections you chose in Activity 4.1a or 4.1b. An abstract is a summarization of a manuscript you would use for a panel presentation at one of the conferences.

_____

_____

_____

_____

_____

_____

_____

_____

_____

_____

_____

_____

_____

_____

_____

_____

_____

_____

_____

_____

_____

_____

_____

_____

_____

_____

_____

Name: _____

Activity 4.3   Campus Student Associations, Clubs, or Groups

Obtain a list of all campus student associations, clubs, or groups. This can usually be obtained from the campus student affairs office. Choose three from the list that interest you the most. Find out the next meeting date and write the date after each group's name.

1. _____

   _____

2. _____

   _____

3. _____

   _____

Activity 4.4 Academic Campus Events

Make a list of all the campus events which have taken place or will be taking place at your campus and/or at a neighboring campus during the past or current academic year. Campus events include table talks, video conferences, symposiums, workshops, job fairs, faculty presentations on special topics, or anything that has educational value. Do not just include criminal justice-related events; include any academic event from any discipline.

_____

_____

_____

_____

_____

_____

_____

_____

_____

_____

_____

_____

_____

_____

_____

_____

_____

_____

_____

_____

_____

_____

_____

_____

_____

_____

_____

_____

_____

_____

5
Back to the Basics: Reading, Writing, Arithmetic, and Research

Many students approach their college courses as separate entities, viewing course material in one class as unrelated to other information and skills they will learn in other classes. If students do not recognize the usefulness of course material to their specific career interests, they often devalue its importance, viewing certain classes as just another step they have to complete to get their degree.

There are problems with this way of thinking. First, students' lack of interest in subject material will often have an impact on retention. For example, if students cannot clearly see the connection between some research concept learned in a methodology or statistics course and their future employment in corrections, they are likely to retain the information only as long as it takes to pass the course. They will often finish this type of class with great relief and the hope that they will never have to use what they learned because, as soon as the grades are in, the material is often out of sight and out of mind, literally. Not only may they need to use what they have learned in these courses in a future job, they are likely to need to use this material in future classes, and retention is critically important. Second, if students are not interested in the material they are learning and fail to see any relevance in the required general education classes, their lack of interest and motivation is often reflected in lower grades. The majority of the students I advise have higher grade point averages in major specific courses than they do in their general education required classes. There are a significant number who even have difficulty completing some of their general education classes, which eventu-

ally stalls their degree completion. Third, if students are attempting to get into graduate school, either law school or a master's program of some type, they will frequently need to demonstrate their proficiency through qualifying examinations in a broad range of material just to be admitted. Once admitted, they will usually have to draw on general knowledge in many classes. For example, good writing skills are extremely important in graduate school when it comes time to write a thesis or dissertation or in law school when it's time to write legal briefs.

Keeping this in mind, the following sections of this chapter are designed to guide you in recognizing the interrelatedness of the course material and how the knowledge can be applied to different classes while you are a student, as well as in your career.

While a Student

One way to view the integration of course material is for you to view your course requirements as pieces to a puzzle. Figure 5.1 provides an example of the many course pieces that make up a degree program.

The goal for you is to find how the pieces fit together. Once the pieces fit together they make a larger picture and, at this point, you should get an *aha* feeling or, to put it another way, the light comes on. This is truly a magical moment and often cannot occur unless you and the faculty alike have this as the ultimate goal. Although you often have no control over whether the faculty used an integrated learning approach, you do have

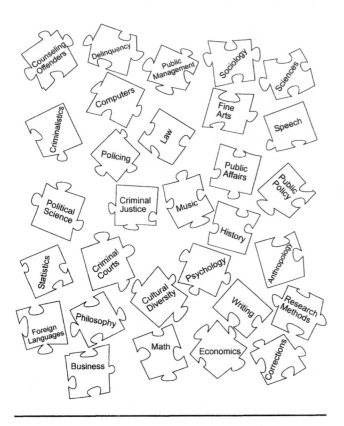

FIGURE 5.1   The Pieces of Your Education

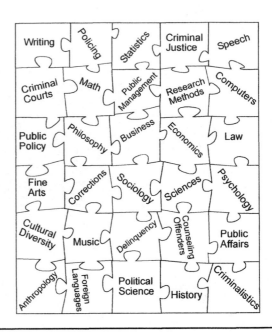

FIGURE 5.2   Your Education as a Completed Puzzle

control over whether or not you, yourself, see the bigger picture and make every effort you can to complete your puzzle. Figure 5.2 illustrates how the pieces of your education can be integrated to complete the puzzle.

Using the exercises throughout this book is one way you can view the bigger picture not only in regards to the importance of your coursework for completion of your degree, but also the significance of the material you are learning as it relates to your future career searches and eventual job performance. The activities at the end of this chapter will help you put the analogy of the puzzle to use, but, before we get to that point, there are some things you should keep in mind that can make the activities as beneficial as possible.

Reading

It's just common sense that anyone in college should be able to read, right? It is also common sense that reading will be required in almost every class you take in college. Therefore, everyone coming into college should be able to read and some type of placement examination for reading proficiency is usually given. What is

often missed in this very basic concept is that knowing how to read and being able to pull from the reading what you need are two very different things. The latter skill is often referred to as reading comprehension.

During your freshman year, you often take courses specifically designed to assist you in reading comprehension for a variety of different materials and disciplines. This is a basic skill that will be used in almost every class you will take thereafter. If you do not learn this basic skill, your inability to comprehend what you read will often be reflected in your academic performance. Therefore, reading, in general, is one of the pieces to the puzzle that, if present, can help complete the puzzle. If absent, however, there will be gaps in your education that are difficult, if not impossible, to overcome.

The level of reading skill required will depend on the course taken. Some texts are easier to read than others. Some even help you identify the main points by highlighting important information in some way or by using marginal notes. Other texts are more difficult to read and your ability to comprehend what you are reading will depend on your use of what you learned throughout your education. You will often be tested on your proficiency in reading comprehension in many courses, both in your major and in required classes, on examinations and assignments.

It is relatively easy to see that reading is a skill that is integrated into most college classes. We will now discuss another general education requirement, writing, a skill used in almost every class you will take as an undergraduate, and as a graduate student.

Writing

Students are frequently required to take one or two writing courses to help them develop their writing proficiency. As with reading, students will have to demonstrate their ability to write in almost every class they take in college, so it should be apparent that writing is another skill that is integrated into other coursework, and a lack of ability in this area will most likely affect your performance. It is another piece of the puzzle and should be viewed as a central one.

The ability to write well will be important on standard college assignments and tests. For example, you may have classes in which the professor uses essay tests to determine your grasp of content and ability to apply this information in other contexts. Professors may also require written assignments, some relatively short and others quite long, that require you to demonstrate your knowledge of the main points. For example, professors may require you to read about what others have written on a particular topic and then summarize the main points, or assign a position paper in which you have to write about your personal opinion on a particular topic. The depth and breadth required on written assignments will depend on the professor's requirements, the level of the course (such as freshman or senior level), and the type of material covered. By your junior or senior year you are usually expected to have a knowledge of the different types of writing styles required, as well as the ability to match your writing style to assignments and examinations given in the course.

Arithmetic

Although students recognize the need to integrate reading and writing skills in other courses, criminal justice majors appear to frequently have difficulty in being able to recognize the need to learn math, often because they do not fully understand its applicability to other courses or to their careers. This may be the result of not including examples from the field of criminal justice in the application of general math concepts. However, it is ultimately the responsibility of the students to make this connection. They should always keep in mind the general question, "How can I apply this concept to my major?" For example, learning the concept of percentages will assist them in turning the raw numbers of a specific crime's occurrence into

data that can be used for comparison purposes to other crimes, cities, or countries. Or, if they are learning about how to calculate rates, they can identify how many ways they can apply it in criminal justice contexts. If they can do this they will be more motivated to learn and retain the material. Instructors are unlikely to teach math concepts in the context of criminal justice. It is the students' responsibility to take the information and think of ways they can use it in classes they currently are taking, in classes they will be taking for their major, and/or in their future careers.

Learning math concepts is frequently a different type of learning for criminal justice students. These classes often require frequent homework assignments and tests, and students must demonstrate their understanding of the material by working problems and coming up with the right answers. It is a process of problem solving, a valuable skill in many different contexts.

Just getting through the required math course often requires problem-solving skills. Some students may need to find study partners, work with a tutor, or meet with the professor regularly. They may have to find ways to deal with frustration and stress, and plan how to manage all of the requirements of the course along with other commitments, both personal and academic. This requires skills in prioritizing and time management, skills that they will need in other classes as well as in their careers.

In a general sense, the key to getting the greatest benefit from the math requirement is to view it as an integral piece of the puzzle. If you can step away from the idea that this is just another hurdle to cross and, instead, find ways to apply the material to your major, you will better be able to recognize the importance of the course material to your education, now and in the future. Many faculty who teach core criminal justice courses will expect you to be able to apply some basic math concepts in some of their classes. For example, in exploring the question of whether crime is increasing or decreasing, you will have to use your knowledge of percentages and rates as well as be able to equalize different data sources in order to answer such a question. Likewise, in a class specific to the courts, you may be required to determine the percentage of felony convictions based on specific variables and then be able to predict future trends. These are just some of the ways in which you can integrate the information learned in required math classes in your major specific courses. This, again, demonstrates the need to see the bigger picture.

Research

Many criminal justice programs require students to complete a research course. These courses are taught from a variety of approaches. For example, some professors focus on the basic elements of research such as completing a literature review and how to design a research study. Other professors focus more on the actual methodology such as determining the best and most appropriate way to sample and the sampling size, developing or selecting an instrument to be used for data gathering, discussing validity issues, and data-analysis techniques. There are times when students may be required to complete two separate courses: one that focuses on basic research concepts and another focused on data analysis through statistical application.

Regardless of the approach used, you may have difficulty recognizing the importance of this material to your career in criminal justice. This is most likely the result of an inability to recognize ways in which you can apply the material or the lack of a requirement for you to demonstrate your ability to do so. You will be more likely to learn the material if you can see the connection between what you are learning in the research class and how this material fits into other courses.

Criminal justice policy development relies heavily on data analysis. In fact, almost all of the basic information you will be learning in your major specific courses is information that was developed based on some type of data analysis. For example, in a class that explores theories of crime, you will be taught about the different theories that are used to explain crime and criminal actions. You will also learn that the original theorists developed their ideas from conducting research such as examining the number and type of crimes committed by individuals who have a specific personality disorder or examining the rate of violent crime in a specified time period before or after an execution. Although these are just two examples, the point is that theorists depend on research. As another example, in a corrections class you will probably be given information relevant to recidivism rates, usually tied to a variety of variables such as type of crime committed, number and type of prior offenses, and length of stay in prison or on probation. This type of information is often used in data analysis in attempts to determine the factors that contribute to a person's chances to recidivate, and to develop a prediction scale.

In a courts class, you are often taught about the various sentencing options available to judges. In connection with this topic, you may be provided information about the success and failure ratings of these various options, all of it based on research. Sentencing options, therefore, are policies based on research.

The examples are numerous. The main point is that the basics taught in the research class will be integrated into other courses you will take. Not only can you use this information to assist you in understanding the content in other criminal justice courses, you can also use research concepts in a variety of other ways. For example, you can use it to critically analyze information given in other courses outside your major such as trends in interest rates, school policies regarding suspensions and dropout rates, pharmaceutical treatments, and psychological testing, to name but a few. You can also use the concepts you learn in research to analyze information given through media sources such as television and news reports. You can look at the facts provided and determine such things as whether it is valid and reliable, whether you would have to have more information on the topic before making a judgment, or whether the source or method of data collection in and of itself makes the information unreliable.

All this said, learning the techniques of research is valuable information not only in the academic setting but for information gathering in general. The material is integrated into almost all other courses you will take and, thus, is an important piece of the puzzle.

Through the information provided in this section, you should now have the knowledge you need to complete Activity 5.1 at the end of this chapter. I will now discuss the multiple ways in which you will be using reading, writing, math, and research in your future career.

In Your Work

In looking at the bigger picture, students need to not only explore ways in which they use knowledge and skills they will gain through their completion of some of the basic requirements, they also need to be aware of the ways in which this knowledge is likely to be used in the various criminal justice professions. A bachelor degree is intended to be more than just specific learning. It is intended that the degree will provide students with a broad base of knowledge applicable to meeting a variety of needs both in the professional realm as well as in graduate school.

It is interesting to note that both law and medical schools accept applications from a variety of undergraduate disciplines including history, English, and the sciences. These schools often are not specifically looking for students who majored in a discipline that was similar to what they will be studying in graduate school. What many of these schools emphasize is a well-rounded education, as well as a well-rounded student who balanced academics with extracurricular activities and interests.

Likewise, employers are often seeking people with specific knowledge and skills balanced with a broad understanding of the basics. For example, someone may be a whiz at understanding the legal code but if he can't write well an employer seeking a professional to conduct investigative work will probably exclude this person as a viable candidate. The specific knowledge taught in major courses is often a body of information that can be learned through work experience, but the basics of reading, writing, math, and research are usually areas that employers expect job applicants to be proficient in when they are hired. The employer is usually not inclined to teach the basics but is generally willing to assist the new employee in learning the ins and outs of the trade. This is not to say that the core required courses are not important. The information that students learn in these classes will not only assist them in learning the specific intricacies inherent in most jobs, but will also help them in determining whether a specific track in criminal justice is an area in which they want to continue.

The following sections will help you recognize the need for not only learning the basics to assist you in doing well in the rest of your coursework, but also the need to acknowledge how the basics can and most likely will be used in criminal justice professions. This information is provided to motivate you to not only do your best in these classes but to retain the information in order to put it to good use in the future. The information is also intended to continue the development of a different type of puzzle. Figure 5.3 illustrates how the pieces of the curriculum requirements can help you as professionals in criminal justice.

Reading

Criminal justice is an ever-changing field. The reasons for creating and changing policy and law derive from current events, whether they be number of and type of crimes committed, types of offender, court decisions, judicial rulings, social events, political changes, or economic fluctuations. All this information develops how we view the world and impacts our delivery of services as criminal justice professionals. The only way we can understand criminal justice as a system is to comprehend what we read, critically analyze the facts and issues, and form our own opinions or positions on the topic.

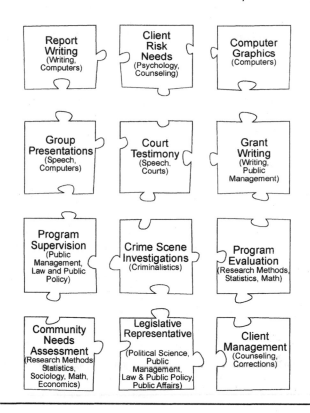

FIGURE 5.3 Establishing the Links between Course Content and Work Responsibilities

Reading is such a critical element of this entire process that it cannot be overemphasized. Keeping up with current events is crucial to any criminal justice professional, whether a line service provider, administrator, politician, government official, or legislative representative. Learning does not end when the degree is awarded. In criminal justice, as in many other professions—such as business and medical occupations—employees need to take the initiative to keep themselves up-to-date on what is happening. A large part of this is taking the time to read the newspaper, books, reports provided in trade journals such as *Police Chief* and *Corrections Today*, and finding up-to-date information on a variety of topics on numerous Web sites. Reading not only helps us keep current but it also helps us with the development of our professional vocabulary and writing skills.

How can reading help with writing skills? Basically, it helps you recognize appropriate and inappropriate ways to phrase, summarize, or paraphrase something. Even if you can't tell someone else how to write well, you can usually tell the difference between good writing and poor writing simply by reading and recognizing the difference. You then can use this knowledge to develop your own writing skills. Reading also helps your writing abilities by providing you with a broader vocabulary. If you learn the correct terms to use through your reading you are more apt to use them in making points in your written and verbal communications.

Keeping current through reading also shows your employer that you are willing to put in the extra effort it takes to move beyond simply being an employee to being a professional. Taking you back to some of the key concepts from Chapter 1, taking the extra effort to learn stems from having a desire and interest in being a criminal justice professional, the heart of the professional. If you are interested in what you are doing as a job you will likely take the time to learn more. I have experienced this passion to learn time and again with students who are invested in their criminal justice major. It is almost as if they can't get enough. They want to learn everything available to them on particular topics. It is usually these students who will make that extra effort once they have a job, and it is usually these professionals who not only find their job to be more than just a job but to be something they actually *like* doing. Making this extra effort is the heart of the criminal justice professional and the effort requires reading.

Writing

Most universities emphasize the development of writing skills and they often require one or more writing classes to be taken during the first two years, the level determined by scores on writing proficiency tests. The goal of these courses is to help you develop versatility in your writing style. This, in turn, will help you adapt not only to the variety of written assignments you will be required to complete in your coursework, but also your ability to write in various professional settings.

Although one would generally expect that students have already developed a certain level of writing skill prior to college that equips them to perform well in spelling, grammar, punctuation, and sentence structure, this may, in fact, be an unrealistic expectation. For a variety of reasons, students may find that they literally have to start over in their writing development. Although often seen as an unwanted or unnecessary requirement, it is best that students develop these skills while they have the assistance they may need readily available to them. Once they are in the workforce, they will most likely find that employers are not inclined to assist them in developing their writing skills through on-the-job training. As with reading, it is expected that new hires will enter employment with an acceptable level of writing proficiency.

A couple of years ago, I was involved in an assessment project in which I gathered information from employers regarding the strengths and weaknesses of new hires. Practically all the employers told me that, although the new hires with a bachelor's degree were well-informed on content knowledge, they were greatly lacking in writing skills. This was a general comment made about all new bachelor's degree hires, not just those from a particular program or college. This information did not come as any great surprise to me, as I have personally witnessed the writing skills of many college students degenerating over the past few years. It is pointless for purposes of this book to get into a detailed discussion of why this may be happening. The point is that employers have indicated poor writing skills as a hindrance to good job performance. Students need to take this information into account when rating their own personal strengths and weaknesses and determine ways in which they can improve their writing skills, if this is an area in which they are weak.

Writing is an integral part of most, if not all, criminal justice jobs. Professionals in all these careers must file reports of some kind. I often think that students are unaware of the amount of paperwork involved in the criminal justice system. Television shows about criminal justice professionals certainly do not emphasize this often mundane part of the job. Unfortunately, viewers come away with an inaccurate perception of what the job truly entails.

Although computer programs greatly expedite a number of the report-writing tasks of the criminal justice professional, people still have to develop reports and depend on their own writing skills to complete the required tasks. The computer programs are of greatest assistance in generating standard forms with blanks that need to be completed and in correcting spelling, punctuation, and grammar errors. The thoughts still must come from the writer.

Yet another factor that you need to keep in mind is that most of the written documents will be a formal part of a record for a particular crime or criminal. This formal record is likely to be read by many people in the system for a long time. For example, once a crime has been committed the patrol officer completes a report, the detectives may follow up with more reports, the probation office may complete a presentencing investigation report, the court pronounces judgment, and an order is filed, at which point all this information may be sent with the offender to the correctional system where more reports are added to the file. Many people involved in the case read this information and poorly written reports will clearly stand out. The criminal justice professional responsible for the report is likely to stand out as well, and the future employment opportunities for this professional are likely to be limited.

It is crucially important that you recognize the importance of writing skills, particularly in the criminal justice professions where accurate, clear, and concise information is so vitally important. A person's future freedom may actually hinge on how information is presented in the documents.

Arithmetic

As was discussed previously, students often do not recognize the importance of math. They commonly view it as a knowledge and skill area that is irrelevant to criminal justice professions. This view is far removed from reality. Whether it be law enforcement, court work, or corrections, math basics are often a needed tool to better understand and perform the work. For example, calculating ratios is important in determining officer-to-geographic workforce distribution. Determining probability for recidivism based on offender or specific variables of the offense is critical in objectively determining sentencing recommendations. Required square-footage-per-prison-inmate impacts decisions made about the maximum number of inmates per prison. All of these examples demonstrate the need for math skills.

Students often tell me that they will not need math because the career they are pursuing does not include a math requirement in the job description. Be that as it may, those very same students may find that there are other tasks required of them once they start the job that do require math. Or they find that they want to pursue a different career track in criminal justice a few years down the road that does require math. Many management and administrative positions require some knowledge of math in order to do planning, budgeting, and program evaluation. Just because graduates may start their careers in entry-level positions does not necessarily mean that a few years down the road they will still want to be in that same position. Employees who want to work their way up the ladder will find that those rungs in the ladder often require other knowledge and skills than those depicted in the entry-level job description.

You are advised to keep in mind that math is fundamental to many everyday responsibilities. For example, when buying a car, you will often have to make a decision whether to take the lower interest rate or the promotional rebate option. In assessing school options for your children, you often want to consider teacher-to-student ratios. When buying a house, you usually want to look at future estimates of property taxes based on previous trends. Math is a part of how you function as an educated consumer. It

is not an irrelevant requirement based on old school thinking.

I often hear students tell me that they do not need to know these basics because there are computer programs and calculators that can figure it all out for them. They still need to enter the correct information and they will still need to interpret the results. Without an understanding of the basics, they will not be able to do this.

Research

Knowledge of basic research principles is important to understanding why we operate the way we do in criminal justice. As criminal justice professionals, we are frequently faced with the need to understand and adapt to changes in the way we operate based on research or the need to conduct research to initiate change or document production and maintain the status quo.

It can often be frustrating for someone to be told by supervisors that changes have to be made in the way things are currently being done. Without an understanding of why those changes are needed, employees often feel frustrated and may be resistant to change. For example, when we introduce new programs to a prison setting, correctional officers may not understand that the change is being made based on research that indicates improved education in persons eighteen to twenty-five years of age decreases recidivism rates by a certain level. The officers may feel that there is no basis for the change or may blame the change on inappropriate administrative decision making or on inappropriate court decisions. Without knowledge that the change is based on research indicating that a positive goal can be accomplished with the addition of an educational component, the officers may be resistant and their negative attitudes can have an impact on inmate motivation to participate. If the officers understand basic research principles, they will be better able to understand why particular decisions are made, provided information about the rationale for decision making is made clear to all involved.

There are virtually countless examples of how research impacts almost everything we do in criminal justice. It not only influences policy decisions and everyday operations of the criminal justice system as a whole, it also impacts the amount of and the qualifications for employment in criminal justice professions. For example, if research indicates that for every officer added to a law enforcement agency, such as border patrol, you can decrease drug trafficking by a certain level, there is likely to be a push to employ a greater number of border patrol officers. Likewise, if research shows that decreasing officer–inmate ratios decreases inmate-to-inmate and inmate-to-officer violence, there is likely to be a push to hire more correctional officers at a particular facility that has been having significant problems with prison violence.

Research can also influence employment qualification criteria and the screening and hiring process. For example, if research indicates that education in diversity lowers the number of lawsuits based on discrimination, there is likely to be an increased emphasis placed on diversity training and education for new hires. There may be research that indicates that a particular protocol for screening of police officer applicants culminates in less turnover and higher job performance. If such is the case, there is likely to be an increase in the use of this particular protocol by law enforcement agencies across the country.

As well as understanding the important role that research plays in operations of the criminal justice system, you should recognize that you, yourself, may have to conduct research of some type in your role as a criminal justice professional. Even as a line service provider you may be asked by your supervisor to gather data from program recipients about their perceptions of the quality of services provided. You may find yourself in a position where you want to ask for funding to initiate a new program of some type and your supervisor requires that you document the need for such a program. This requires research. For example, a police department may want to ask for increased funding for more patrol officers. The city council is likely to require that data be gathered to support the request. Or a correctional facility may be in danger of losing funding of its job-training program and the superintendent of the facility asks that data be gathered to support the continuance of the program. This all requires research, and just because you may be in a line service position as an entry-level employee rather than an experienced administrator does not necessarily mean that you will not be required to do research of some type.

The ability to conduct research is valuable and is often a highly marketable skill. In Chapter 4 you learned how to make yourself more marketable. A working knowledge of the many uses of research is definitely a marketable skill. Entering criminal justice employment as a new hire knowledgeable in research will most likely assist you in your future opportunities.

The information contained in this section was provided to equip you with the tools you need to complete Activity 5.2, which is designed to help you understand how you can use the basics in your career.

Personal Experience

I was one of those students who had trouble seeing the bigger picture. I was so totally interested in learning discipline-specific content from the required core courses that I often gave short shrift to the need for getting a well-rounded education. At the time, I could not understand why math and research fundamentals were requirements of the program. I also often felt the requirements for lengthy topic papers and book reports were unnecessary. At the time I was completing my undergraduate work, I had no intention of going to graduate school. Overall, I did not understand that the continued development of skills in reading, writing, math, and research would be so crucial to my work and education in criminal justice.

As life goes on and people mature and experience new things, goals and interests can change. That is what happened with me. I wanted more challenge and more administrative responsibilities. I also wanted to continue my education with a master's, and possibly, a doctorate. This change in personal goals led to a geographic change so that I could be in a community with the graduate program I wanted and a job promotion I was interested in. It was at this point that my knowledge, skills, and abilities also had to change. Although I previously had experienced job duties requiring a great deal of report writing, I now found that the knowledge and skills needed to complete graduate work as well as administrative duties were different. I also found that I needed to put to use my previously learned research fundamentals, mainly for program evaluations used in year-end reports. I was now also responsible for managing program budgets. As I moved through my graduate education and advanced into other administrative positions, I found that I was relying more and more on the fundamentals of reading, writing, math, and research. These knowledge and skill areas were needed for a variety of job responsibilities including grant writing, budget development, management, program evaluation, and review and revision of written reports. These educational basics were also needed in my graduate courses.

My experience serves as an example to others that the fundamentals we learn in our undergraduate education are necessary in a variety of future life ventures. The more we recognize their importance while we are undergraduates, the more likely we are to remember this knowledge and quit viewing these requirements as hurdles to get past and, instead, view them as valuable tools for the future.

Activity 5.1   Curriculum Requirements as a Puzzle

Using either the course catalog or an advisor's checklist, write down all of the classes you have taken or will be taking to complete your degree. You may not know what your general elective courses will be at the time you complete this activity, but you do know what the general education and major course requirements are. Next, design a puzzle that indicates a piece for each course you have or will be taking. Make the puzzle piece sizes appropriate to what you consider their importance to your education. It is suggested that you make a draft of your puzzle design before you start cutting the pieces because, as you design your puzzle, you may find that you want to make some of the pieces more central to the design in order to indicate their importance. The example of a puzzle design provided in the chapter should give you an idea of how this activity is to be completed. The space provided below can be used to draw out your ideas for the puzzle. It is suggested that completion of this project be made on larger, thicker paper.

Activity 5.2   Pieces of the Future

Following up on the work you have already done in Chapter 3, find five to ten job descriptions (not announcements) of employment opportunities in criminal justice in which you may be interested. Make a list of the knowledge, skills, and/or abilities required in each position. Make a new puzzle that includes a piece for every requirement in the job descriptions. Highlight or color all of the pieces for which you feel a course you have taken or will take fulfills the requirements and note on the puzzle piece which class meets this criteria. Next write a brief reflective essay on what you have discovered through this exercise. The puzzle example given in the chapter should help you get started.

6
Addressing Challenges

A career in criminal justice can be exciting and rewarding work. The sense of accomplishment you can get when a breakthrough has been made in changing future criminal behavior or in preventing or solving a crime is unrivaled in most professions. Working day-to-day with people from all walks of life, whether they be victims, offenders, or common citizens just looking for assistance from someone they feel they can trust, can instill a sense of pride in what you do for a living. Personally, I feel there is no more honorable profession nor more fulfilling work than a career in criminal justice. That said, it is important for you to recognize that you will most likely be faced with certain challenges that go hand and hand with the benefits of such a career.

This chapter will focus on four specific topic areas: working for a bureaucracy, working with colleagues, working with the public, and knowing yourself. This is not to say that there aren't more challenges to the job than these four. However, by focusing on these areas, it is expected that you will reflect on how these challenges may impact you personally. As in my previous discussion of the importance of being able to make informed decisions, the emphasis here is on educating yourself, as a future criminal justice professional, about factors to keep in mind when starting your career.

Working for a Bureaucracy

What is bureaucracy? For purposes of discussion here, it is the rules, regulations, record keeping, and hierarchy of authority considered necessary to carry out prescribed functions. Bureaucracy forms the structure under which an organization operates. Many of the jobs criminal justice graduates will be seeking are in the public sector. Working for a government bureaucracy is not the same as working for a private for profit or even a private nonprofit organization, although the latter is more likely to involve government work as its primary funding source. For one thing, government employment often has a detailed set of policies and procedures that regulate everything from position advertisement, screening, and hiring to salary and promotion to communications to day-to-day operations. Secondly, the bottom line in government employment is commonly efficient and effective delivery of services, whereas the bottom line with private agencies is usually profit. Third, the scrutiny under which government services are provided and, consequently, the work performed by the employees, is frequently at a much higher level than work performed by private agencies, especially those not funded through government moneys. All three of these elements are actually tightly linked and are essential to our understanding some of the challenges of government bureaucracies.

Over the years, for a variety of reasons, people have associated the term *bureaucracy* with negative aspects of government work. The term is frequently linked to another, equally negatively perceived term, *red tape*, and the general public often associates their negative perceptions of red tape with the concept of bureaucracy. In a sense, this develops a cyclical negative perception. Is there a basis on which this perception has developed? Of course there is! Ask most anyone what agency they associate with red tape and a *typical* bureaucracy and many will name their local department of motor vehicles. Depending on who you ask, others will name the welfare department or the Internal Revenue Service. If asked why they feel the way they do, many will tell you that the policies and procedures hinder the operations of the agency, bogging it down to the point where efficiency and effectiveness cannot be accomplished.

If asked about their perceptions of bureaucracies and red tape, will criminal justice employees respond with similar comments? Probably yes. New employees may hear comments during their training periods such as "We go by the book here" and "Rules are rules—follow them!" Employees, new and old alike, may express frequent frustration with this line of thinking. One way to cope with or overcome these feelings is to develop an understanding of why government agencies operate the way they do. This awareness may help reduce the frustration and encourage more contentment among employees and, consequently, higher job performance.

First, it is important to recognize that the criminal justice system serves enormous numbers of people. Without some type of set procedure based on clearly defined rules and regulations and accurate record keeping, level of service would be left up to the individual discretion of the employee. It doesn't require much thought to see that this could have disastrous results. Second, there is the fact of public scrutiny. All government work is subject to scrutiny, but criminal justice services receives a great deal more than most other disciplines. Media representatives frequently want to find answers to *why* some action was or wasn't taken. It is their job to explore these topics and inform the public. Who else would do it, if not the media? If employees are following procedure then they, personally, are less likely to be publicly criticized. This is not to say that the procedure itself, or the agency proponents of the procedure, won't be scrutinized and possibly heavily criticized. But following procedure is often a protection for the government employee. Third, government agencies and their agents can be sued. The formality of the rules and regulations that government employees frequently tire of may someday come to their aid to defend them against liability. The more employees can understand the benefits as well as the challenges of working within a bureaucracy, the more likely they are to accept, and even appreciate, the need for structured rules, regulations, and record keeping.

Are there employment opportunities for criminal justice graduates who would rather not work for a government agency as a result of their negative feelings toward bureaucratic organizations? Of course, but there may be tradeoffs that have to be taken into consideration. Not everyone who works in criminal justice is a government employee. For example, many private companies have employment opportunities that provide services similar to those typical of government work. Private security is only one example. Major department stores, banks, insurance companies, and housing developments are examples of some of the places where graduates may seek employment in the private sector while still being able to stay in the field of criminal justice. Does this necessarily mean there won't be set procedures? Of course not! However, there may be fewer levels in the chain of command and there may be greater opportunities for initiative. Changes will most likely occur faster and frequently smoother, but there may also be less job security and fewer protections for the employees.

There are also numerous employment opportunities for criminal justice majors with private nonprofit agencies. These providers often are partially or completely funded through government moneys and, thus, have to abide by government regulations concerning employment announcements, selection and hiring procedures, and client services. However, these agencies may have greater opportunities for individual initiative, changes may occur more quickly and smoother, and the number of levels in the chain of command are often fewer than traditional government bureaucracies. The bottom line is usually efficient and effective provision of client services. As with private for-profit agencies, job security may be a concern, but for a different reason. The funding of these agencies is commonly term-restrictive, meaning that each year or two, seldom longer, the agency will have to reapply for funding and, depending on numerous variables, may or may not be able to continue providing services as in the past.

All three categories of employment discussed (government work, private for-profit, and private not-for-profit) have their benefits and challenges. There are many more differences in these three employment environments to take into consideration than what has been provided in this brief discussion, and you should educate yourself on these differences before making choices about employment opportunities. Private as well as public organizations all have varying levels of bureaucratic organization. Just because you choose to go into private employment does not mean there won't be red tape. It is up to you to reflect on how you would respond to working with the level of rules, regulations, and record keeping often required in government bureaucracies. This is yet another reason why educated choices combined with reflection are so important when it comes time to make decisions about future career opportunities.

Working with Colleagues

Some of you may have heard the phrase "You can't pick your family; you are born into it." To a certain degree, this same concept applies to what may be termed your work group. The work group is the other employees with whom you will have regular contact in the performance of your duties. These can be employees of the same agency with which you work or they can be employees of a collateral agency with which you have regular contact. For example, probation officers may find that their work group consists not only of other officers from their own office, but also the police, prosecutor, public defender, and judge working on a particular case. Therefore, the work group may be stable, such as other probation officers within the division, or can be variable based on professionals involved in each case.

When you are seeking employment, you are usually interviewed, sometimes by one individual and other times by a group of agency representatives, but you usually do not get to meet the people you will be working most closely with until after you start the job. The situation can result in any number of scenarios, but, in general, you may find that, although you are a good fit for the job, you are not a good fit with the other employees of the agency. It is always hoped that the fit will be good but, personalities being what they are, there are common occurrences when strained relationships can interfere with job performance, job satisfaction, and may even result in workforce turnover.

As a criminal justice professional, you are placed in an interesting position in that you will most likely not only have to work on building positive relationships with colleagues within the office, but will also have to build positive relationships with an ever-changing work group. As you can imagine, this is no easy task. Add to that the fact that in criminal justice work, perhaps more so than in virtually all other occupations, new employees have to prove themselves before two-way relationships can be established. New employees are often seen as outsiders and are frequently put into situations where their integrity, knowledge, skill level, and abilities are being put to the test by their colleagues. How they perform in these test situations will frequently determine whether the agency colleagues or work group accepts them, or, if not acceptance, then at least the development of a working relationship.

Added to all this is the fact that professional positions in criminal justice come at all levels from line service personnel, such as patrol officers and probation officers, to judges. Do people in certain positions view themselves as being superior to others? Absolutely! It may be difficult for a probation officer to argue a point with a judge (in closed chambers, of course) because

a judge may see herself above a probation officer. If the work group is to accomplish its goals, everyone will often have to step out of the *level* of their roles (not step out of their role) and address each other as equals.

As an example to illustrate these points, think about the plight of a recent graduate, a female, twenty-two years of age, who is starting a position as a probation officer. This officer has been thrown into the responsibilities of her job and will have to sink or swim. Not only is she having to learn the standard operating procedures of the agency, she is also trying to build positive relationships with her colleagues, including her supervisor, other officers, and support staff. She is also in a position where she will have to develop good relations with the police because it is they whom she will have to rely on to get information about clients, their cases, and any violations. She will also have to rely on the police when faced with high-risk situations. At the same time, she is having to develop positive relations with attorneys from the prosecutor's office and the public defender's office as well as private attorneys representing various clients. Attorneys provide a valuable source of information and can be supportive or unsupportive of her efforts in working with the clients, which can culminate in poor relations with the clients, which, in turn. can hinder her effectiveness as a supervising officer. She is also going to have to develop positive relations with the judges, eventually winning their trust in her recommendations when it comes to sentencing or violations. In the midst of all this, she will also have to develop positive relations with the support staff of all these professionals in order for her requests for information to be granted in a timely manner. Developing these positive relations is no small feat and sometimes takes years. Add to this the fact that the work group is constantly changing and, because of transfers, promotions, and terminations, her own agency's work group is often unstable.

So how does she develop positive working relationships with colleagues and deal with the work group personalities in a way that will build the bridges necessary to accomplishing goals? First, she has to establish herself as a professional, and oftentimes this depends on her ability to demonstrate not only her content knowledge but her proficiency in the basics. She is, in fact, building her reputation. Second, she should tread lightly, at least in the first year, in order to get a feel for how people operate, the individual personalities she will be working with, and how best to accomplish what she needs to in order to perform well.

Third, she will need to be clear about her own personal goals and ethical standards so that, when she is faced with tough decisions, she will know what to do. Last, she needs to recognize that some colleagues are simply not collegial in their interoffice interactions. It is a fact of life that some people are just more difficult to get along with and, at this point in her career, she may need to consider developing a way to work with such people *through* others or *around* them.

There are countless ways in which you can interact with others and develop working relationships. It is important that, as a criminal justice professional, you learn to adapt your relationship-building styles to meet the specific situation.

Working with the Public

As a public service employee, you enter a profession in which you will most likely have regular contact with diverse groups of citizens under enormously varying situations. Criminal justice professionals work directly *with* victims and offenders and/or work indirectly *for* them, such as through contacts with counseling organizations, job-training programs, educational providers, religious organizations, and the media, to name but a few. You will also be communicating with the family and friends of victims and offenders alike.

Due to the basic nature of the job, as a criminal justice professional you will need to have good communication skills in order to perform well. Also, you will often encounter members of the public during difficult times. Dealing with such situations on a daily basis can become frustrating and stressful. Having to constantly change your communication approach to meet the needs of those involved in a situation can be extremely challenging. You will have to develop the skills necessary to become a situational communicator, changing your style of communications to meet the specific needs of a variety of individuals.

In a more general sense, it is important for you to recognize that much of the public has preconceived notions of criminal justice employees and how they perform their jobs. How you perceive criminal justice in general and employment responsibilities in particular is greatly influenced by the media—television shows, movies, and news coverage. Most people also form their perceptions in the same manner. Consequently, their expectations of the role criminal justice professionals play may be unrealistic, which can cause negative reactions if a professional does not look, act, or respond as the public expects. For example, correc-

tional officers are frequently portrayed as mean-spirited and unintelligent. Using that stereotype to deal with real-life officers would be inappropriate. Stereotypes could be provided for virtually every profession portrayed in some way by the media. Unfortunately, this situation can create many problems for the criminal justice professional.

Recognizing that you are going to be treated in terms of such stereotypes is a first step in figuring out ways to deal with the public. A second step would be for you to help inform those you are serving about what your responsibilities and limitations are in order to encourage reasonable expectations. It is important not to reinforce stereotypes when you interact with the public. You should, instead, interact on the basis of what you have learned as well as following the set procedures of the agency for which you work.

Knowing Yourself

Having read the previous three sections, which described some of the challenges inherent in criminal justice professions, it is now up to you to determine how all of this is likely to impact you personally. Recent graduates come into these careers with different backgrounds, coping strategies, problem-solving skills, interest areas, tolerance levels, communication skills, and so on. All of this affects how each of us is likely to react to particular challenges. Thinking through your probable reactions and recognizing your personal challenges is one of the steps to becoming a professional.

When you consider working in a bureaucracy, a useful way to determine whether or not you could work well in this environment and enjoy your job is to examine three common differences between government employment and private for-profit work: (1) chain of command, (2) paperwork, and (3) set procedures. Although there are other differences, the focus will be on these three primary areas. Government employment often requires its employees to follow a chain of command with all communications and, frequently, it utilizes a top-down approach. Those with authority give directives that move down the chain, and those at the lower levels in the chain are expected to submit questions, concerns, and feedback to the next higher level in the chain. Second, government organizations often require a great deal of documentation. This, in turn, means that employees often have a significant amount of paperwork to complete, often involving not just form completion but narrative report writing as well. Third, with many government jobs the manual of operating procedures is detailed. This means that there is likely to be a rule or regulation governing almost all of the employee's duties and responsibilities. Trying to understand the procedures can be a monumental feat in and of itself, so following the procedures in every situation can be frustrating. Although well-justified in their creation, these set procedures are often seen as obstacles to individual initiative and roadblocks to change. The bottom line in determining whether or not you are a person who could work well in a typical bureaucratic government organization hinges on these three general areas. Activity 6.1 is designed to encourage your personal reflection with respect to these areas.

In developing positive working relationships with colleagues, it is important to explore how you interact with people and how people interact with you. For example, when faced with a situation where you feel your ideas are not appreciated, do you become angry and withdraw? Or do you try to force others into going along with what you say should be done? Or, maybe you are a person who gives up easily when others disagree with you and then later feels resentment toward them. There are many ways in which you interact with others. Knowing your personal interaction and relationship-building skills, and honestly recognizing the strengths and weaknesses of your skills, will help you in determining ways to improve your communication skills and accomplish your goals.

Another aspect of working with colleagues is knowing whether you can accept feedback and/or criticism well. As a new employee, there may be situations that arise when you have not performed your duties the way others think you should. It may be your supervisor who criticizes what you have done or not done or it may be a colleague. Are you a person who sees criticism as a personal attack or do you accept it as feedback that can be used to improve your performance? Criminal justice professionals often deal with a great number of colleagues because they have frequent contact not only with people in their own office but with other professionals in the system, and there may be times when these colleagues criticize something you have done or left undone. Its important to try to separate feedback from personal attacks and learn from the experience. For example, a judge may find some report you wrote lacking and may tell you that you better learn to write or you won't be in the job for long. Such a statement from a judge can be intimidating but it is important that you find out what is lacking from the report so that you don't make the same mistake again. Or, if the judge is literally criticiz-

ing your writing then you better figure out how to improve your writing skills. Perhaps the structure of your writing is not clear and concise. Although this is something you should have learned in your college classes, it is a skill you can still improve through instruction. When a colleague criticizes your work performance it is important to (1) be aware of how you are reacting to this information, and (2) determine if or how you can use the feedback.

As a criminal justice professional you are going to be working with people who have different degrees of power, from a coworker to department heads to elected officials. It is important to adapt your style of communication to each specific situation. Your ability to do this will depend on a number of things, such as your past experiences in communicating with diverse groups of people and your own confidence in your knowledge, skills, and abilities.

How well you work with the public will also depend on your own personal style of communication. However, it also depends on other factors. We all have preconceived notions that influence how we react to different situations. For example, somewhere in our lives we may have developed a strong personal dislike of drug offenders. As a criminal justice professional, this personal feeling can have an impact on how we interact with drug offenders. Being aware that we have a set of preconceived notions that may influence our interactions with the clientele we serve is a first step in acknowledging how these attitudes and beliefs affect our interactions. Reflecting on why we feel the way we feel and why we interact the way we do is an important process in becoming a professional and performing our job duties to the best of our abilities.

Working with the public requires adapting your personal style of communication to the situation. For example, some police officers have difficulties shifting their approach from communicating with offenders to communicating with victims. In these situations the victims come away from the interaction feeling as if they were interrogated. They may even feel that they were not only a victim of the crime but a victim of the system as well.

How to interact with the public is not something students can learn all about in school. Developing this skill will most likely depend on experience, but how well you interact with different people and situations will also depend on your ability to reflect on those interactions, recognizing what went right and what did not go well and determining ways to improve in this area. In knowing yourself, much of this comes down to recognizing your interpersonal strengths and weaknesses and reflecting on how your own personal experiences have impacted your perceptions of people in general, and crime, offenders, and victims in particular.

Much of criminal justice work is relatively stressful in comparison to other occupations. Knowing how you deal with stress is important. You are likely to feel frustration with how the criminal justice system works or doesn't work, how professionals in the system do or do not do their jobs, and how you are accepted or not accepted as a professional in the system. Knowing how you deal with this type of frustration is important. Activity 6.2 is designed to assist you in knowing yourself.

Being aware of your personal strengths and weaknesses means more than just being aware of whether you have the requisite knowledge, skills, and abilities to perform a particular task or fulfill specified job duties. It also means being in touch with who you are as a person: how well you adapt to change, how you accept feedback and criticism, how you work through frustration, whether you are more productive working in a group setting or working individually, and how you deal with stress.

Personal Experience

I never took the time to reflect on issues like these either before or after I decided to major in criminal justice nor before I started a career in this field. I did not know that finding a good fit between who I was as a person, the job responsibilities and duties, and the work environment was so necessary to my continued interest and enjoyment of the job. I take partial blame for this because I never took the time to educate myself on the realities of the various careers in criminal justice or reflect on how I was suited for them; but I also feel that the college program in which I was enrolled could have provided greater support in individualized career advising.

There have been some challenges along the way with my personal career choices. On reflection, I was not suited for police work but I was a good fit with correctional employment. I am also finding that I am well-suited to my more recent career shift to academia. I often tell students that who I am as a person fits better with jobs where I can have individualized professional working relationships with people. I also tell them that this is because I am a social service agent at heart. I have learned that this means that I am interested in and derive pleasure from assisting people in finding ways to fulfill their needs, whether that be aiding offenders in locating employment opportunities, continuing education, and finding housing or in providing assistance to students in course advising and career planning.

To find a fit in career, it was important to learn more about myself. I discovered that I needed to reflect on why I felt the way I did when faced with work-related frustrations and stress, why I reacted to particular cases and people the way I did, who I felt most comfortable working with and why, and what I was willing to change about myself in order to better adapt to my career and what I was unwilling to change. This process has taken time (the development of maturity) and regular and honest personal reflection and self-awareness.

Activity 6.1   Government or Private Sector Employment

The differences between public and private sector employment are numerous. It is important that you reflect on whether your personal goals, interests, values, strengths, and weaknesses fit better with government or private sector employment. Making choices often involves determining the best way to balance the benefits and challenges. Using the information in this chapter as well as brainstorming with others or individually, make a list of the general differences between employment with the government and employment in the private sector.

Government Employment   **Employment in the Private Sector**

_____   _____

_____   _____

_____   _____

_____   _____

_____   _____

_____   _____

_____   _____

Next, based on these differences, write a brief essay on which sector of employment you feel better meets your goals, values, strengths, and weaknesses as well as which would fit you personally.

_____

_____

_____

_____

_____

_____

_____

_____

_____

_____

_____

_____

_____

Activity 6.2   *Getting to Know Yourself*

Go to your college career placement office, complete a self-awareness survey, and obtain the results. Below, state the name of the test or survey you completed and the date taken. Next, summarize what you found out about yourself and how that information may apply to your future work experiences.

Name of Test or Survey: _____

_____

_____

_____

_____

_____

_____

_____

_____

_____

_____

_____

_____

_____

_____

_____

_____

_____

_____

_____

_____

_____

_____

_____

_____

_____

7
Politics, Politics, Politics!

Many criminal justice job opportunities will be government positions for the city, county, state, or federal government. Even employment in the private for-profit or not-for-profit realm often has some link to government involvement through the funding source or through the network with whom the employee will be working. For example, private criminal law attorneys will be networking with prosecutors, police officers, probation officers, and judges. Knowing who you are working *with* is as important as knowing who you are working *for*. When you begin your career, it is important that you understand the relevance of this basic concept.

The importance of finding ways to work well with colleagues both within the agency as well as those in the vast network of professionals who make up the criminal justice system was discussed in the previous chapter. In this chapter we will examine the role that politics plays in most, if not all, criminal justice jobs. For purposes of this discussion, we will examine the influence of politics in two contexts; one being the more literal use of the term with elected political positions and the second being the looser use of the term applied to intra- and inter-office interactions. We will also explore how politics influences not only government employment but private for-profit and not-for-profit agencies as well.

Elected Leaders

Saying that politics influences the criminal justice system is probably an understatement. It is more realistic to say that politics *rules* the criminal justice system. For one thing, many of those with decision-making power are elected officials such as prosecutor, sheriff, judge, mayor, and legislative representatives. In the broadest sense, the influence of politics goes all the way to the president of the United States, who nominates Supreme

Court justices and cabinet secretaries. Decisions made by elected officials and their appointees, aides, and advisors mold and direct how the criminal justice system does business, influencing every realm of the system from policy to service provision to employment opportunities as well as impacting such agencies as the Drug Enforcement Administration, the Federal Bureau of Investigation, Bureau of Alcohol, Tobacco, and Firearms, Customs Service, Immigration and Naturalization Service, and the Bureau of Prisons.

It never ceases to amaze me how many students do not understand the basic identifiable tenets of the political parties. This is of particular concern to me considering the fact that many criminal justice students will become government employees directly or indirectly under the leadership of some elected official. To better understand how politics plays such an enormous role it is important to go back to some of the basics most students should have learned during their primary years of education.

In the United States, there continues to be two major political parties, Republican and Democrat, although there are third parties that gain in popularity from time to time such as the Progressive Party, the Green Party, and the Reform Party. Political parties often have identifiable agendas, at times very diverse and at other times similar in nature. These agendas set goals and objectives that party supporters hope to achieve by having their elected officials in power.

Certain words or terms have come to be identified with the Republican and Democratic parties that have been used, in the most general sense, to describe the parties' political agendas. For example, Republicans are identified as conservative and Democrats as liberals. Translating these labels into criminal justice agendas, numerous examples can be given. On the issue of illegal drugs, conservatives generally support law enforcement initiatives and tougher sentencing whereas liberals generally support prevention and treatment initiatives. As another example, conservatives, overall, focus on initiatives that emphasize public safety, whereas liberals focus more on protection of individual rights.

How does all of this translate into political influence over the criminal justice system? It goes back to political agendas. The party in power will support legislation that represents its agenda. For example, during President Reagan's (Republican) time in office (1980–1988), one agenda was tough on crime and "war on drugs." Drug enforcement has been categorized as a conservative agenda whereas the democratic agenda tends to focus more on prevention and treatment. During this time period, when the Republicans were in power, enforcement was emphasized. Keep in mind that we are looking at an example in the most general sense. This is not to say that prevention did not receive attention. During this same time period, First Lady Nancy Reagan promoted the "just say no" initiative, which can certainly be considered a preventive approach to the drug problem. However, due to the focus of President Reagan's administration, federal agencies involved in drug enforcement grew, sentencing became more punitive, and the numbers of drug offenders in correctional facilities rose dramatically. This example illustrates the influence of politics on the criminal justice system and is not meant as a statement about the Republican agenda.

Presidential power and its influence on criminal justice extends all the way from Supreme Court nominations to cabinet appointments to fiscal allocations and so on. Supreme Court justices have a tremendous impact on the criminal justice system, whether it be policing, court, or correctional operations as illustrated in such cases as Miranda v. Arizona (1966), Gideon v. Wainwright (1963), Mapp v. Ohio (1961), Terry v. Ohio (1968), and Estelle v. Gamble (1976), to name a few. There have been shifts in the conservative and liberal approaches taken by the Court over the years, aligned, to a certain degree, with the political agenda of the party in office. However, it is also important to remember that a justice seat is a permanent position. Therefore, even when political parties shift, the Court maintains its political leanings based on the justices that continue to sit on the bench.

The President can also influence policy through budget allocations for criminal justice agencies and their operations. Through the budgeting process, funding is provided to accomplish goals and objectives of favored policies. As an example, we can again look at President Reagan's drug enforcement agenda. During

his eight years in office the funding to pay for the "war on drugs" went from $1.5 billion in 1981 to $4.7 billion by 1988. By 1993, after President Bush's four-year term, carrying forward the "war on drugs" initiatives, federal spending to combat drugs was $12 billion (*CQ Researcher*, 3/19/93). From 1982 to 1993, the number of federal justice employees went from 94,555 to 162,202, a 71.5 percent increase. The federal agenda is often replicated on a state and local level, depending on the political party in power at the time. For example, the number of state justice and local employees increased from 341,010 in 1982 to 548,139 in 1992, a 60.7 percent increase, and state justice expenditures increased 154.2 percent (see *Bureau of Justice Statistics*, NCJ-148821). If the party at the local and state level is the same as the president's, then the agenda is likely to be similar. If the party is different, then the agenda may differ as well.

Therefore, it is important that you, as a future criminal justice professional, recognize the influence of politics on the state, county, and local levels. Similar to the federal political structure, in state government, the governor is responsible for appointing his or her own department heads. For example, the governor can appoint the secretary or commissioner of corrections. This person is likely to share the governor's agenda. It is quite feasible that the agenda of that office is likely to change, to a certain degree, each time the political party controlling the governor's office changes.

On a more local level, changes in political positions, such as the prosecutor's and sheriff's offices, can greatly impact employment opportunities for future graduates. New jobs may be created while others may be eliminated or duties and responsibilities changed to better accomplish the goals and objectives of the elected official. Job security is sometimes at risk, depending on the state code, which regulates whether or not the newly elected official can dismiss staff and bring in his or her own people.

It is important not only to examine how politics can directly impact employment in criminal justice through elected positions, but also to recognize how politics can indirectly affect employment as well. For example, many city mayors are elected officials. These officials can have a great deal of influence over appointment of the police chief. Therefore, although the police chief may technically not be an elected official, the position is still heavily influenced by the political party in office.

How does local politics directly or indirectly impact criminal justice students considering a career in this field? The agendas of the elected officials can impact the duties and responsibilities of the criminal justice employee. For example, if the agenda of the local prosecutor is to crack down on drunk driving, then it is likely that the police will emphasize prevention and enforcement of this offense with check points and mandatory arrest policies. They are also likely to change their patrol patterns to focus on particular areas in the city where drunk driving is more likely to occur. The prosecutor's decision to crack down on drunk driving may have been a reaction to a vehicular homicide wherein a drunk driver crashed his truck into a car of five teenagers on their way to the local high school football game, killing all five. For purposes of this example, let's say that it is later determined that the drunk driver had four prior traffic offenses involving alcohol and was currently driving on a suspended license. This incident will probably receive wide media coverage and the public is likely to express its frustration and anger, perhaps blaming the prosecutor's office for not pressing for a felony conviction on the previous offense or the police department in not preventing such an occurrence. Mothers Against Drunk Driving (MADD) may become involved in encouraging policy changes. At this point the prosecutor, an elected official, is likely to recognize that public sentiment is favorable to greater sanctions. To gain the support of the public during the next election, the prosecutor may support policies to create tougher sanctions and greater involvement of the police department in preventive strategies. Hence, based on public sentiment concerning a particular case, the person elected as prosecutor is likely to promote changes in police department and prosecutor office policies and operations, which, in turn, can change the duties and responsibilities of various criminal justice professionals.

As another example, let us take a look at domestic violence. Perhaps there has been a tragic instance of domestic violence that has resulted in widespread media coverage. For example, perhaps a woman and her four-year-old son were beaten to death by the husband. The media releases information that the police had been dispatched to the home on seven prior occasions but no arrest had ever been made, and the woman was not given information about alternatives available to her, such as safe houses and shelters, or, perhaps, these alternatives are not available in the community. The mayor, prosecutor, and police chief are likely to take some heat from this event. A task force may be created to recommend policy changes, and this situation may force the mayor, prosecutor, and police chief to crack down on domestic violence. This could then translate into mandatory arrest of offenders

or removal of victims from the home. The new policy then changes the duties and responsibilities of the police officers dispatched to the home. The new policy may also create a need for better or more access to shelters. A task force will probably be created in the prosecutor's office specifically to address domestic violence. Ultimately, the public outrage over such a crime can result in an expression of dissatisfaction with those currently in decision-making positions, the mayor, the prosecutor, and the police chief. If these officials do not respond actively to the crime, the voters are likely to develop a negative view of their capabilities and this can impact voting results during the next election.

In both of these examples, changing agendas, which create new policies and procedures, have an impact not only on operations of the police but also on the prosecutor's office and the correctional system. Duties and responsibilities of employees within these systems are likely to change, such as a special unit to address domestic violence may be created in the prosecutor's office. Alcohol counseling and anger management classes are likely to receive more emphasis and correctional workers, such as case managers as well as probation and parole officers, may be expected to assess and refer clients to community services or address the issues themselves. Funding may even be made available to contract out with counseling professionals to address these offender populations, which can expand employment opportunities within private for-profit and private not-for-profit agencies.

These examples also illustrate how special interest groups influence elected officials' agendas. These groups, such as Mothers Against Drunk Driving and other advocacy groups, can play a major role in influencing policy changes. Their support or lack of support of elected officials can impact these officials' current and future political careers. These groups may be very vocal about their opinions, and their positions are often brought to the general public through the media. The general public then forms their opinion of how the criminal justice system as a whole is performing, and judge the competence of particular elected officials on the basis of what they read and hear through the media. Their opinions will likely influence how they vote in the next election.

Many examples could be given but the point has been made. So, what is the message for you, a student considering a career in criminal justice or social service? Understand the agendas of the political parties, whether it be on a national, state, county, or local level. This will entail reading news reports, listening to or watching news coverage, and attending town meetings and other events that give voters a chance to meet the candidates. Take an interest in educating yourself on what is occurring in the world, not just in your own backyard. Next, find out the agendas of those in decision-making positions and take the time to think through how the agendas of elected officials and others with decision-making power can impact you personally in your job search and future career. Activity 7.1 is designed to help you better understand the impact of politics on career opportunities.

It is equally important that you consider previous trends in criminal justice policy to better project career opportunities. What are some of the criminal justice policies that have been created in the past ten years? Does it look like there will be a heavier emphasis on enforcement five or ten years from now? What political party is likely to be in power and what changes to the criminal justice system are likely to occur? What direction does the Supreme Court appear to be taking in regard to criminal justice issues? Answers to these questions will help you plan your continuing education and identify career options. Hiring criteria, such as knowledge, skills, and ability requirements, are likely to change based on the answers. The question to ask yourself is, "Will you be ready for these changes?" Activity 7.2 will assist you in determining trends in hiring practices in a field in which you are interested.

Office Politics

Although still often referred to as "politics," the intra- and inter-agency interactions in which employees engage and the results of these interactions have a different meaning from the political influence on the criminal justice system based on agendas of elected officials and their appointees and advisors. The phrase, "it's who you know more than what you know that will get you ahead," refers to "office politics." Graduates, as new employees, may find that both intra- and inter-agency interactions are often based on office politics. This can be both confusing and frustrating to the new employee.

Office politics can greatly impact operations of the agency. If collegiality and teamwork is strongly supported and rewarded, then job satisfaction and job performance is likely to increase and job turnover is likely to decrease. However, an office environment that allows, or even encourages, manipulative and self-serving behaviors on the part of its employees is likely to have employees that blame poor job satisfaction, lowered job performance ratings, and high turnover on office politics.

Criminal justice employees are likely to interact with a wide range of other professionals as they carry out their duties, which means that you should recognize that some of the negative aspects of office politics extend far beyond the office within which you may be employed. Although, in general, much of government work is highly regulated with extensive operating policies and procedures, how the system actually functions often depends on relationships within and between agency workers. This may not be the textbook version of how a system runs, but it is often reality and, perhaps, an unwanted necessity.

You may have heard the phrase, "You can't always follow the book." There may not be another occupational field in which this is truer than in criminal justice services. The circumstances and persons that comprise a criminal event are individualistic. Add to that the fact that each professional involved in processing this event has a tremendous amount of discretion and decision-making power, and you have the elements for variation rather than for consistency and routinization. Next, add in the fact that many of the key players in the system will have regular contact with each other in future cases, and you have the ingredients for individual case decisions being made on prior interactions that are not relevant to a specific case.

To a new employee this way of operating may be very confusing and frustrating, which will most likely require you to have several different types of coping strategies. For one, you might make it perfectly clear that you will operate only by way of the book, with no variation. This will most likely work to some disadvantage in the future when you need or want some special compensation made on a particular case due to special circumstances. Secondly, you may try to please all the people all the time, but we all know from our own personal experiences that that is virtually impossible. This will most likely limit your bargaining power in the future because the other key players in the system will not know where you stand on certain issues and will most likely not trust you. Third, you might choose to play it as close to the book as possible, while at the same time observing how the system operates, how the key players interact, and how best to accomplish your agency's goals while maintaining your own personal ethical standards. The third option is, of course, preferable for those of you who want to continue your employment in criminal justice. Although the choice may appear to be a simple one, it often is not.

For one thing, turnover is relatively high in many criminal justice occupations. Therefore, changes will occur in work group relationships, both intra- and inter-agency. It is also important that you recognize that the criminal justice system is fluid in nature: it is greatly influenced by both internal and external factors that can impact office politics. For example, equal employment opportunities called for dramatic changes in the composition of the workforce in many criminal justice occupations. With the changes in gender distribution came changes in office politics—how individuals interacted with each other.

How do you know that you will have the adaptation skills necessary to work with the politics of the criminal justice system? Reflect on how you have adapted to new academic or work environments in the past and identify your strengths and weaknesses in these personal adaptation skills. The activities in the previous chapter should assist you in determining your personal strengths and weaknesses in relationship building. Office politics is a reality. Recognizing this and learning ways to deal with this reality in a positive way will increase the likelihood for greater job satisfaction and performance.

Politics and Employment in the Private Sector

Some criminal justice graduates will find government employment as city, county, state, or federal professionals, but many of you will find employment in the private sector, either immediately on graduating or after a term of employment as a government worker. Based on the potential for private sector employment, it is important for you to recognize the influence that politics has on the private sector.

When I use the term *private sector*, I am including private for-profit agencies such as private security and investigation firms, as well as private not-for-profit agencies, such as counseling services provided solely through government contract. The private security firm makes its profit from pay received by private companies for services rendered. For example, providing loss prevention for major department stores, doing background investigations for private companies, and providing security for major sporting events. Private for-profit companies may manufacture security equipment used by private security agencies or sell the equipment to the government. For example, some of the latest technology being manufactured for airport security has been developed by for-profit companies.

The private not-for-profit counseling agency selects its own employees but commonly pays salaries with monies from the government for providing a specific service. In this case, the agency is not in the business of making a profit, does not have stock options, and, in many cases, does not collect fees from its clientele. Salary increases are received as a result of an increase in the government contract, not as a result of increased client fees and collection.

It is important for students to recognize that politics still has an enormous impact on employment opportunities and responsibilities in the private sector. For example, if a governor's agenda is to address drug crime through prevention and drug treatment, there is likely to be more funding made available to private not-for-profit agencies that have experience in drug treatment. Professionals in these agencies would be serving the offender population, but not as government employees. Private for-profit agencies may create drug prevention programs for the employees of private companies. For example, a large car manufacturer may pay an agency that specializes in drug prevention strategies.

As another example, a political incumbent may have an agenda to crack down on crime through stricter community corrections sanctions. This agenda may facilitate the creation of electronic devices used to track offenders in the community. Private companies may manufacture these devices and sell them to the government or contract with the government to supervise offenders in the community through use of these devices. Private not-for-profit agencies may contract with the government to provide community surveillance as well. The point to be made is that even employment in the private criminal justice sector can be impacted by political agendas.

It almost goes without saying that office politics operates in the private sector just as it does in any other context. However, it is important to recognize that office politics in private sector criminal justice occupations can become even more convoluted due to the nature of criminal justice services. Private sector employees will be interacting on a regular basis with government employees. The challenge lies in adapting interactions to the differing goals and expectations of the private and public sectors. The bottom line for some private agencies is profit. The bottom line for many private not-for-profit agencies is continuance of government contracts. Both profit and continuance of government contracts will most likely depend on positive evaluations of quality services. The people making the evaluations are likely to be government workers or, possibly, private contractors, perhaps from a local university. Understanding the politics of how decisions are made about continuing government contracts or paying for company services is the lifeblood of the private sector. Some of this will depend on the larger arena of government politics, for example, the agendas of elected officials, and some of this will depend on relationships between government decision makers and private sector providers. It is important that you keep this in mind when considering employment opportunities in the private sector. Activity 7.3 is designed to provide you an opportunity to gain a better understanding of the relationships between private sector providers and the government.

Personal Experience

I entered government employment as a state probation and parole officer with little to no understanding of how politics influences the day-to-day activities of a line service worker. I did not even know that the governor appointed the commissioner of corrections. I also did not understand how the change in governors and, consequently, the change in commissioner of corrections, could impact my job responsibilities. I had probably learned, in some class, that governors could make political appointments of key criminal justice personnel, but I never stopped to think about how this could impact criminal justice employment opportunities as well as job responsibilities. Reflecting on my experiences, I now understand why some of my responsibilities changed with time. I can also better understand how the changes in policies impacted the entire criminal justice system, which eventually trickled down to my level. On a more local level, the changes that occurred, for example, in the county jail system as a result of new policies resulting from a change in leadership, also impacted my job: more people were being placed on probation due to a lack of space in the jail, thus increasing my caseloads.

Through the years I have also learned a great deal about office politics. Adapting to changes in leadership within the office as well as to changes in coworkers as people entered and left their positions has always been a challenge. Personalities come into play when trying to build working relationships and have

productive teamwork. I learned that a great deal of the job stress I experienced was not so much from the clients I worked with but from office politics. Differences in perspective and opinion between coworkers and bosses mattered more to me when I was younger than it does today. I always thought that I had to convince people to see it my way when, in fact, others were trying to do the same and there was little effort to meet in the middle. With experience and, perhaps, just getting older and more mature, I learned that I was not always right (hurts the ego sometimes) and that, in working together, the synergy of teamwork often had more productive results.

I have also come to accept that politics is here to stay. Elected officials will come and go and so will their platforms. I have learned that, regardless of who is in the decision-making positions, I can keep my personal values and beliefs intact and find ways to work with the alternatives available to me.

I have also learned that, no matter where I work, public or private sector, office politics exists. My strategy of working with this reality is to keep the goals and objectives in mind with whatever job I hold. For example, when I taught parenting classes for those required by the court to complete the classes, the goal was to stop abusive and neglectful parenting behavior and actions. The objectives were to have the parents develop knowledge, skills, and abilities to achieve this goal. My role was to provide the information in such a way as to promote the learning process. Keeping these goals and objectives in mind I was able to focus on my role and disregard any negative impact office politics could have had on my being able to fulfill my job duties and responsibilities, such as colleagues devaluing the importance of the program based on their personal opinions about child abuse and neglect.

References

Cooper, M. H. (1993). *War on drugs: The issues. CQ Researcher*, March 19, 1993.

Lindgren, S. A. (1997). *Justice expenditure and employment extracts, 1992: Data from the Annual General Finance and Employment Surveys.* (U.S. Department of Justice, Office of Justice Programs, Bureau of Justice Statistics, NCJ-148821).

Activity 7.1   Elected Officials and Employment

Select a criminal justice department, office, or agency that has an elected official at the top such as the prosecutor's office, the sheriff's department, the courts, or the governor's office. Identify the policies that regulate hiring and termination of employees of the agency. State or county codes or the personnel departments for the state or county may be a place to find this information. Next, summarize the information following the format below.

1. What agency, department, or office did you gather information on?

    _____

2. What elected position is in charge of the agency, department, or office (such as prosecutor, governor, sheriff, etc.)?

    _____

3. In what employment positions can employees be changed at the discretion of the elected official?

    _____

    _____

    _____

4. Which, if any, employment positions cannot be filled by people appointed at the discretion of the elected official?

    _____

    _____

    _____

Name: _____

Activity 7.2   Hiring Trends

Select a criminal justice career in which you may be interested. Research the hiring trends specific to that career for the past ten years. In the space provided below name the career and provide information relevant to the number of hires for that position over the past ten years. For example, if you are interested in a patrol officer position in a particular city or county, find out how many officers the agency has had, on an annual basis, over the past ten years. Next determine how many positions have been filled for patrol officer, on a year-by-year basis, in that particular agency over the past ten years. The city or county personnel office is a possible resource. This type of information for a number of federal departments (DEA, FBI, ATF, or border patrol) is likely to be found on the Web. Information about prosecutor and public defender positions will likely come from the county personnel office. Information about a state correctional position, be it officer, case manager, or counselor, is likely to come from the state personnel office.

1. Career: _____

2. Number of employees in the career over the past ten years on an annual basis:

   Year _____   Number of Employees _____

   Year _____   Number of Employees _____

   Year _____   Number of Employees _____

   Year _____   Number of Employees _____

   Year _____   Number of Employees _____

   Year _____   Number of Employees _____

   Year _____   Number of Employees _____

   Year _____   Number of Employees _____

   Year _____   Number of Employees _____

   Year _____   Number of Employees _____

3. How many employment positions have come open and been filled over the past ten years?

   _____

Activity 7.3   *Employment in the Private Sector*

Select a private for-profit or not-for-profit organization that provides criminal justice services of some type in your local community. Contact it to gather the following information:

1. Name of organization: _____

2. List of criminal justice-related services or goods for which the organization has a government contract:

   _____

   _____

   _____

   _____

3. Number of employees in the organization who are paid partly or fully through government contracts:

   _____

4. Title of employment positions that are funded through the government contracts:

   _____

   _____

   _____

   _____

   _____

8

The Importance of Networking

Networking has been referred to directly and indirectly in previous chapters, mainly in the context of the relevance of networking for future employment opportunities, but it has also come up in reference to politics and the need for understanding intra- and inter-agency relationship building. For purposes of my discussion here, the network referred to is the criminal justice system consisting of police, courts, and corrections providers. Networking will be defined as the inter- and intrarelationships between public and private sector agencies that provide services in the criminal justice system. This includes both verbal and written communications.

In this chapter you will examine, in detail, what is meant by the term *networking* in the context of criminal justice employment and operations. Throughout the chapter, you will be examining the relevance of networking from a micro perspective in opening the door to career opportunities as well as the need for networking in day-to-day operations of the criminal justice professional. You will also be exploring networking from a macro perspective, examining how networking in criminal justice requires developing communication links with other disciplines such as social work, psychology, and business.

Networking for Career Opportunities

The information provided in Chapter 4 established the premise that networking while you are a student is critical to opening the door not only for the first job held after graduation but also for future career opportunities once some experience has been gained. Whether seen as fair or unfair, opportunities for jobs often stem as much from *who* you know as *what* you know. Using the network of who you know more than what you know in order to be favored for a position can have signifi-

cantly negative outcomes, as it should, and the civil service protocol was created to avoid such unsavory tactics. However, as most of us are aware, letters of recommendation are usually required for many job applications. These letters are based on who you know and their evaluation of you as a person, a student, and an employee. Without this information, selection panels would only have college transcripts and applicant self-reported information on which to base a hiring decision.

It has been said that letters of recommendation should not be given much weight in the final decision because applicants will only request recommendations from people they feel confident will have only good things to say. However, the individuals in the network who provide recommendations are often known to each other and reputations have been established. A positive recommendation letter from someone who is known by the network of professionals as having good judgment in determining whether a job applicant is a good fit for a position will go a long way in providing credibility for the job candidate. Likewise, the network is usually aware of those who make recommendations for just about anyone and ultimately does not give much consideration to whether the applicant is qualified for the position. In this example, although the author of the letter makes a positive recommendation, it is not given much credibility. This said, you need to understand the network of professionals within your occupational choice as well as their reputations before asking for letters of reference.

You may be wondering how you develop this understanding when you have not had a job in the criminal justice system. It goes back to what was discussed in detail in Chapter 4—making yourself marketable—and part of that is making the connections with criminal justice professionals while you are still a student. This can entail any one or more of a number of options usually available to you including volunteer work, community practicums, internship placements, attendance at professional conferences, participation in campus events, and attending career fairs. Getting to know the people who are employed in various criminal justice jobs helps you to develop an understanding of how the network operates, including the communication flow, the selection process, and who are in decision-making positions that can have an impact on your employment opportunities.

It is important for your career that, after hire, you continue to develop your understanding of the importance of networking. Once in a position, you, as a criminal justice professional, are given a greater opportunity to network with other professionals and these contacts may lead to promotions or career changes.

It is important to keep in mind that your reputation is likely to follow you wherever you go. I have always found it interesting that criminal justice professionals within a community, state, or even at the national level are a relatively small network. Of course, this depends on the type of position held as well as the state in which you work. I have personally come back into contact with people I have not communicated with for ten or more years and found out that we are now serving together on some national task force. A particular phrase you may have heard fits this discussion: your reputation precedes you. In establishing network links it is important to realize that what you do and say today can follow you for a very, very long time. That can work either for or against you, depending on your reputation.

As a student, how do you make networking benefit you? Most importantly, always be professional in your interactions. Being professional can mean many different things, but in the context of this discussion it means presenting yourself in the best possible way. How this is done will depend on the situation and task at hand. In general, being professional usually means being timely in both your appearance as well as in task completion. It also means quality work, whether it is written assignments, verbal presentations, or teamwork. Quality work entails clarity and conciseness while displaying a comprehensive understanding of the topic. Quality work is also error free and usually demonstrates the time investment and critical thinking required of the task at hand. Being professional also extends to verbal communications with colleagues (fellow students), supervisors (people who oversee volunteer or internship placements or current employers), and professors. These are the people you

are most likely to come to for letters of recommendation or who will be contacted through background investigations. It is also through your contacts with these people that you will start developing your reputation as a professional.

To illustrate the importance of this point, I will provide a couple of fictional examples. Mike is a second-semester junior who has taken three prior classes with me. He is now under my supervision for his internship placement. In prior classes, Mike has consistently been on time for class as well as timely in turning in all assignments. He has displayed excellent communication skills, both written and verbal. He has shown good leadership skills when given a group assignment and he was evaluated, by other students, as being a good team player during some out-of-class activities that required sharing the workload. The supervisor at the police department where he is completing his internship has nothing but good things to say about his appearance, his task completion, and his initiative in taking on more work than is assigned to him. Mike has come to me, his college professor, for a letter of recommendation in his pursuit of an internship during the summer with the Federal Bureau of Investigation. I write a positive letter of recommendation, I provide a positive reference during his background check, and I contact an FBI recruiter I know to ask if she can also put in a good word for Mike.

Lucy's situation is different. Lucy has also taken three prior classes with me and is a second-semester junior currently doing an internship in the community. Lucy frequently showed up late for classes and missed approximately 20 percent of the class sessions. She frequently came to me to ask for time extensions for her written assignments. Her communication skills, both verbal and written, are marginal. Her current internship supervisor rates her as satisfactory or below satisfactory for each skill required. Lucy has asked me for a letter of recommendation because she wants to get into the same program as Mike. I refuse to write a letter of recommendation, but she is able to obtain the required three letters through other channels. During the background check, the program investigators contact me because I have served as Lucy's academic advisor for the past three years. I provide them with factual information about her academic performance.

In these examples, Mike presented himself as a professional not only in an academic setting but in a work setting as well. Lucy, on the other hand, did not present herself as a professional in either setting. You can readily see that the career opportunities for Mike are much greater than they are for Lucy. Although these examples may appear simplistic in nature, I can personally attest to the fact that I have experienced such variability in student professionalism every semester. You need to recognize that your reputation as a professional starts while you are still a student and your contacts with your professors as well as your internship supervisors are the start of your networking in the criminal justice system.

Networking on the Job

Establishing your networks while you are a student will enable you to widen the door of career opportunities. Establishing your network after beginning your career in criminal justice is important not only for promotions or career opportunities but also for fulfilling your current job responsibilities.

Similar to needing recommendations on graduation in order to get that first criminal justice job, you will most likely need letters of recommendation for job transfers and references for promotions. You will usually be asking people you have networked with as part of your current work for these letters. Once again, the nature of these recommendations and references will generally depend on the reputation you have built for yourself. My advice is the same: continue to present yourself as a professional in all your interactions with colleagues, supervisors, and the public. Now your reputation is not solely based on how you performed in an academic setting but also on how you perform in a professional setting. I have known many people who could do the book work and were excellent students but who had difficulty in transferring their knowledge into the real world of work in the criminal justice system.

Networking as a professional entails communication. In Chapter 5, the importance of communication skills was emphasized. In that chapter we focused on good written and verbal communication skills. It is equally important to remember that people develop a perception of you from your style of communication, in other words, as much from what is said as from what is left unsaid. A couple of simple examples will illustrate this point.

Mary is relatively new to her work as an adult probation officer, having been in this position for only six months after graduating with her bachelor's degree in criminal justice. She has been assigned a presentencing report on an offender convicted of three counts of trafficking in cocaine. In exploring the past criminal record of this individual, Mary is confused about some of the

information in police reports. She places three phone calls to the investigating officer but does not receive a response. Mary is frustrated with what she sees as a lack of cooperation and sets up an appointment with the investigator's supervisor to discuss the situation and voice her opinion of the poor way the investigator wrote the reports as well as his failure to communicate with her. What do you think of Mary's networking skills? What is Mary's style of communicating? How else could she have handled the situation?

Joe is an investigator with the prosecutor's office. He has also been on the job for about six months. He has been assigned the task of gathering information from police officers involved in a particular case as well as the probation officer who has worked with the client in the past. Joe finds out the shift the police officers are currently working and calls during their shift time to set up a convenient time to talk. Joe has left several messages for the probation officer but has not heard back. Joe drops by the probation department during business hours and inquires about the availability of this particular officer. He discovers that the officer is on vacation for two weeks and that is why the officer has not been returning messages. Joe decides that the best course of action is to put his request into writing and have it waiting for the officer on her return with specifications about when the information will be needed. What do you think of Joe's networking skills? What is Joe's style of communicating?

Although simplistic, these examples illustrate how a person's style of communicating can impact his or her ability to network with other professionals. These examples are also given to make the point that how you network with other professionals will likely have long-term consequences. If Mary continues to go to supervisors each time she does not get what she wants or needs, she is likely to alienate the very people she will have to return to time and again. Although jumping rank may be necessary from time to time, it is better to carefully select those times after having exhausted all other avenues for networking.

It is important to choose our battles carefully. Many people have long memories and are not forgiving of those who they feel have slighted them in some way. Mary, just starting as a probation officer, is going to have a difficult time gaining the cooperation of the police when she needs it if she continues to complain to supervisors. Being a probation officer requires regular contact with the police in order to get reports, gather insider information on the activities of clients, and request backup for particularly hazardous situations. Mary needs to build her network within the police department in order to do her work. Without their cooperation she is likely to have high job stress, poor job performance, and terminate her position prematurely. Joe, on the other hand, is likely to build positive networks with other professionals because he tried to accommodate the varying schedules of the police officers and he did not go to the probation officer's supervisor when the officer did not respond immediately to him. Instead, he followed up with an office visit and a letter that clarified exactly what he needs when the officer returns from vacation. Joe showed consideration in his interactions. This style of communication is likely to be remembered in a positive way and Joe is likely to receive cooperation when he has to return to these professionals for assistance with other cases.

The way you network with other professionals will affect both your ability to perform your job and future career opportunities. Personalities being what they are, you are likely to run across people you have to network with even though you do not share similar values or communication styles. There are likely to be other professionals you will be working with that you will not like for one reason or another. It is important to always be professional in your interactions and to choose your battles wisely. If you are going to go to the wall over something, make sure it is worth it and that you understand the consequences. There are battles you may choose to fight which, in the long run, may hurt you professionally but that you feel are worth the cost. Being true to yourself and your profession is more important than a job promotion, although at the time it might not seem like it. If you have done a good job of networking in the past and have a good reputation with other professionals in the system, you are likely to be able to weather a few storms without too much personal damage. But building your network and establishing your reputation takes time, so it would be wise to try to stay away from career crippling battles when you are just starting out.

Networking with Professionals in Other Disciplines

Criminal justice work is an occupation that is likely to put you in regular contact with professionals of other disciplines, such as education, social work, counseling, and job-training fields, so professionals in these fields are likely to become part of your network. Similar to establishing your reputation with colleagues within the criminal justice system, having your name and

work in good standing with these other disciplines is equally important.

How much contact you have with people in other fields will depend on what type of criminal justice job you hold. Police officers are likely to be in fairly frequent contact with social workers and school teachers concerning reports of child abuse and neglect, student substance abuse and behavior problems, and truancy and dropout status. Juvenile probation officers are also likely to be in regular contact with these other professionals as well as psychologists and other mental health professionals who are also working with youth. Probation officers are also likely to have frequent contacts with employers in the area and the state-operated employment office, as well as other professionals in disciplines that serve client needs. Court personnel, such as investigators and attorneys, are also likely to have contact with professionals in other disciplines as they prepare their cases, develop their witness lists, and seek alternative sentencing options. Activities 8.1 and 8.2 are provided to assist you in better understanding networks in criminal justice.

It is important to recognize that, although sharing information within the criminal justice network, such as between police, court, and corrections personnel, is generally expected, establishing relationships within this broader network of professionals may be more difficult. First, confidentiality issues often come into play. For example, the mental health professionals are likely to release only limited information without a consent from the client and, even with the consent, are likely to filter the information they provide. The same may be true for social workers and school personnel. Second, it must always be kept in mind that everyone is busy with their own job responsibilities. Taking the time to discuss a particular client with someone outside their own discipline may not be a priority. Third, people in these various fields, in general, will be concerned with how client information will be used. This concern may inhibit the flow of information.

However, there are things that you can do to overcome these obstacles to networking. First, be clear on what can and what cannot be kept confidential by other professionals. Ask for a copy of the consent form and the agency's regulations on confidentiality. This shows the other professional that you are taking the time to learn the rules of the game and are willing to work within those rules rather than try to bypass them. This will go a long way to establish your own reputation as a professional as well as strengthening the network you will most likely need to use in the future. Second, calling ahead to schedule a convenient time with other professionals is usually preferable to just walking in the door and expecting them to make time to meet with you. Again, this shows that you respect them and are trying to work within their time constraints. Third, be as honest and up-front as possible in respect to how you are going to use the information you are asking from them. If they feel that you have deceived them for purposes of gaining information, they are not likely to communicate with you in the future. Your reputation as a professional has been jeopardized as well as your ability to fulfill your job responsibilities.

Career Changes

Developing networks with professionals in other disciplines is not only critical in helping you to fulfill your current responsibilities as a criminal justice professional. These links may also prove fruitful if you decide to change careers. There are a number of occupations in other fields outside criminal justice that provide services to similar populations but in a different context. For example, some case manager positions within the public and private school systems work directly with students who have behavioral problems and high truancy rates. Educational specialists provide services in many of the jails and prisons across the country as either government employees or contracted providers. Some job-training programs are geared specifically to provide services for offender populations as are many substance abuse programs. The opportunities for individuals who have experience and interest in working with offender populations in contexts outside traditional criminal justice occupations are numerous. The networking you do while a professional opens the door to mid-career changes and second career options.

Personal Experience

As a state probation and parole officer, I rapidly learned the importance of networking with a broad range of other professionals who, directly or indirectly,

had some involvement with a particular case and/or offender. When I started the job, I did not have a clue about the extent to which the network would reach. I certainly had not learned about the importance of networking in any of my classes, so my awareness came only through on-the-job experience. I learned that the network of a probation and parole officer included bail bond agents, counselors, educators, police, court staff, prosecutors and public defenders, job trainers, housing representatives, utility company staff, church representatives, employers, and many others.

Although it took me at least two years to figure out who to call and when in various situations, I also figured out that developing a network is an ongoing task. There was turnover in all agencies, which created a need to develop the network of people on an ongoing basis. There were also new services that had to be brought into the network. There were unusual cases that came up that created a need for me to reach outside the local network to intra- and interstate resources. As well as constantly fluctuating, I learned that the network can become very broad in nature.

The network not only assisted me in fulfilling my duties and responsibilities, it also became a valuable resource when I decided to change jobs while still working with offender populations. I knew where the jobs were, what the responsibilities of employees within those jobs were, and when positions would become available. Through the network I had also established my reputation as a professional and had numerous references available on request.

Did this happen overnight? Of course not! As with most things in life, I found that you only get out of it what you put into it. In the case of networking, I discovered that the time investment was well worth the effort as it assisted in developing networks that could be useful in my work with clients as well as to my personal benefit in the future.

Name: _____

Activity 8.1   Network Chart

Chart out the network that could be used specific to one particular career area. Be sure to include both public and private sector providers. Don't write this out as a narrative but instead diagram the connections. You can either hand-draw the diagram or create it through a computer program. Remember that the links of a network are usually multifaceted. Be sure to include on your diagram which career area you used for this project.

111

Name: _____

Activity 8.2   Contacts in Network

For the exercise in Activity 8.1, make a list of all the agencies and identify an employee within each agency who provides relevant services to offender populations. For example, if the employment security commission (or unemployment office) was in your diagrammed network, contact the agency and find out who provides training classes or employment services specific to offender populations.

Agency Name	Contact Person
_____	_____
_____	_____
_____	_____
_____	_____
_____	_____
_____	_____
_____	_____
_____	_____
_____	_____
_____	_____
_____	_____
_____	_____
_____	_____
_____	_____

9
Ethics

All students should have learned, or will be learning, through their academic coursework that there is a tremendous amount of individual discretion used in the decision-making process in criminal justice work. Countless policies, rules, and regulations for procedures have been established to guide decisions made throughout the criminal justice system. These have been put in place to standardize operations, to provide consistency, and to limit abuses of discretion. Ethical standards have also been established to guide the various professionals in provision of services. Each of the occupational groupings within criminal justice—police, courts, and corrections—has its own code of ethics used for this very purpose. However, even with all of these mechanisms in place, due to the very nature of criminal justice work, discretion can be used inappropriately and unethical behavior can occur.

What should you know about ethical standards, your own personal ethics, and how these fit with your chosen profession? In this chapter you will take a closer look at what is meant by the term *ethics* in the context of criminal justice professions, and you will explore various applications of the term through the use of scenarios. This will allow you to bring to the decision-making process your own personal ethical standards and to explore the consequences of the decisions you make. You will also explore the importance of ethics in the development of the public's perception of criminal justice occupations. Finally, you will look at some of the ethical challenges new employees, as well as experienced professionals, face in this field. The goal of this chapter is to provide you with an opportunity to recognize some of the challenges specific to criminal justice occupations with respect to ethical behavior and to better prepare for making ethical choices. The activities at the end of the chapter will assist you in accomplishing this goal.

Ethics Defined in Context

Ethics has generally been defined as moral principles, a code of conduct, good compared to evil, right compared to wrong, and standards of behavior. Some of these terms suggest a personal belief system (moral principles, good and right compared to evil and wrong), while others imply a clearly defined description of expectations based on profession (code of conduct and standards of behavior). Regardless of the phraseology, the general meaning of the word is most likely to be the same. This becomes evident in looking at various codes of ethics, such as those for law enforcement, policing, sociology, psychology, and public administration, which can be found in many introductory texts. These codes typically describe expected and acceptable behavior on the part of employees or professional association members.

The underlying theme of the codes that dictate conduct in the criminal justice professions involves integrity, honesty, trustworthiness, impartiality, equity, and exemplary personal character. Oftentimes there is a ceremony for new employees, such as police officers, probation and parole officers, and correctional officers as well as members of the bar, at which they swear under oath to uphold the code. They are often required to keep a copy of the code with them at all times and to refer to it for guidance. In other words, the message is that the code is to be taken seriously, used regularly, and upheld.

One aspect of the ethical codes in criminal justice that is perhaps most different from those in other professions is the frequent reference to conduct expected of employees in their private lives. Many of the codes contain a section that states, in general terms, that their off-duty character and conduct must be beyond reproach. Therefore, criminal justice professionals not only swear to uphold a code to guide their work behavior but also to guide all their behavior. To do so, it would be expected that personally held ethics are in line with professional expectations.

Personal Ethical Standards

Our personal description of ethical behavior may contain certain elements that are different from stated codes particular to specific professions. Why? In a word, individuality. Each of us has our own history that we bring with us to the profession. This includes how we were raised as a child as well as the influences of those close to us during our youth such as peers, church groups, school associates, and others participating in extracurricular activities. All of these people can impact how we perceive the difference between right and wrong, good and evil, and how we develop our personal moral principles. What I consider right or good may be different from what one of my colleagues perceives as right or good because of our personal histories.

Do personal ethical standards remain the same over time? Probably not. Beliefs in what is right and wrong are likely to change with time. What I considered right or good when I was twenty is somewhat different from what I perceive as right today. As adults, we continue to develop our principles of morality as we have different experiences. Who you are today, and what your personal ethical standards are, is a composite of all your life experiences, and you will most likely alter some of your personal ethics as you continue to grow through experience and mature.

Just as it is likely that we may alter some of our ethical beliefs with time and experiences, it is equally likely that some moral principles will carry us through all our lives. For example, "do unto others as you would have done to you" is a basic moral principle that many of us are taught while very young and we try to adhere to that principle throughout our lives. Another principle that many of us learn while young and that, in numerous variations, is included in many of the codes is "equality for all." This is an example where a phrase can become a principle and follow with an ethical standard depicted in a professional code that guides our interactions with the public.

By the time you are a student in a college program you have already developed some ethical standards learned as moral principles while you were young. What is important is that you reflect on these beliefs and determine whether they are something you want

to adhere to today or whether you need to eliminate or modify some of them. It is one thing to have a belief but it is another to act on it. For example, if we say we believe in honesty yet cheat on our taxes because we think that everyone else does, then we are not living by our own ethical standard. If we espouse equity but base decisions on race, gender, or religion, then we are not acting on our ethical principles.

When a profession has specific expectations of its employees based on a code of ethics and the guiding principles of that code differ from our personal beliefs, or our actions as a professional differ from the expectations, we are not being true to ourselves or our profession. This can lead to a variety of consequences, ranging from conflicts with colleagues to poor job performance to corruption and illegal behavior. The activities at the end of this chapter are provided to assist you in reflecting on your personal ethical standards as well as to compare those standards with the code of ethics for your chosen profession.

Scenarios: Dilemmas in Ethics

Knowing where you stand with your own personal ethics is critical when entering criminal justice professions. The very nature of the job will entail situations where temptations to engage in unethical behavior will be numerous. The following scenarios are provided to help you think through various situations you may encounter as a criminal justice professional and to encourage you to consider what the specific ethical dilemma is that must be faced and what decision you would make as well as the consequences of that decision. The scenarios can be used in individual reflection as well as class discussions or group exercises.

Scenario One

Many probation officers are responsible for monitoring illegal substance use by doing urine screens. Pat is a probation officer with two years experience on the job. The agency policy and procedures require random urine screens of all probation clients at least every three months and more frequently based on a case by case, as needed basis. The policies also require that documentation of screening results be kept in case files and accurate notes kept by the officers as to when and under what situation a urine screen was collected and sent to the lab for analysis. Policies also require that a letter be written to the prosecutor indicating the presence of an illegal substance on any probation client who tests positive. Pat has a caseload of 125 clients. Through her years she has been very careful to adhere to these requirements for all clients. She considers her personal approach to probation as a combination of surveillance and assistance to meet client needs. Through her contact with the prosecutor's office she has discovered that there appears to be no consistency in the decisions to go forward with a probation violation based on a dirty urine screen. Sometimes the attorneys at the prosecutor's office will file a petition to revoke and other times they won't and she can't determine on what basis they are making their decisions. One of her clients is a single mother of three children, all under the age of ten. This client has recently gotten a full-time secretarial position at a local real estate office, which provides her an opportunity to get off of welfare for the first time since she became a parent. The crime for which she was placed on probation was possession of cocaine. A random urine screen determines the presence of marijuana. Because Pat is concerned that a petition to violate may be forthcoming if she reports this to the prosecutor's office, she makes the decision to shred the lab results and to note that the urine screen was clean.

> *Is* there an ethical dilemma and, if so, what is it? For example, what moral principles come into play? (integrity, honesty, trustworthiness, impartiality, equity, and/or exemplary personal character)
>
> Do you feel that Pat was right or wrong in her approach? Why?
>
> What would you personally do?
>
> What is the basis for your decision?

Scenario Two

Steve is a patrol officer with fifteen years experience. He works in a mid-size department with 400 officers, in a city with a population of 150,000. Over the years he has had excellent job performance evaluations, has received three awards for excellence in service, and, from all accounts, gets along well with other officers. But Steve's personal life is a mess. His twelve-year marriage ended in a hard-fought custody battle for the couple's three young children, and Steve was not awarded full or joint custody but was awarded occasional weekend visits and every other holiday. His ex-wife was awarded the family's new van, the house, and half the money in savings. Steve must maintain payments on both the van and house mortgage as well as pay $900 per month child support. Through the di-

vorce proceedings, it was discovered that there had been numerous incidents of domestic violence at the home although no police reports were on record. It was also discovered that Shelia, Steve's ex-wife, had been treated in the emergency room seven times over the past five years for dislocated joints in her fingers, a broken nose, and stitches on several occasions. Since the divorce, Steve has been running into some financial difficulties for failure to pay credit card charges with purchases he made since the divorce and the credit companies are threatening to turn Steve over to the collection bureau with the threat that there is likely to be wage garnishment. Steve has not discussed any of these personal difficulties with anyone at the department. However, records indicate that Shelia had called the department to talk with Steve's supervisor four times in the three years prior to the divorce. Shelia states that she told the supervisor about the domestic violence and Steve's violent temper. The department has also received phone calls from various creditors who leave messages for Steve to call them back although none of the creditors have asked to talk with Steve's supervisor to date.

> Is there an ethical dilemma and, if so, what is it? For example, what moral principles come into play? (integrity, honesty, trustworthiness, impartiality, equity, and exemplary personal character)
>
> Would you say there are ethical problems with the way the department has handled the situation?
>
> What would you suggest should be done?

Scenario Three

Rob is a public defender with five years experience. He works in a mid-size community with a population of 300,000. Rob had been a public defender in another state for seven years before his current job and in yet another state for four years before that. Rob is a single man with no children. The public defender's office was satisfied with Rob's work performance during his first two years, but for the past three years his supervisors have become more and more dissatisfied. Rob has consistently been missing appointments with clients, has shown up late for several court hearings, and has totally missed five scheduled preliminary hearing dates in the past year. Both judges and prosecutors have contacted Rob's supervisor, Elaine, several times to report their dissatisfaction with his work performance. Elaine has guaranteed all of them that she will address the issue with Rob and that there will be no more problems. What the judges and prosecutors don't know is that Elaine and Rob have been having an affair for the past three years. Elaine is married with two children. What is also unknown to the judges and prosecutors is that Rob has a substance abuse problem with cocaine. Rob's colleagues in the public defender's office are aware that Rob and Elaine are having an affair and are also aware of Rob's substance abuse problem. They are unsure how to handle the situation because they are concerned that if they complain to Elaine, due to her relationship with Rob, they will either lose their jobs or be given the least favored work assignments, so they have not said anything.

Is there an ethical dilemma and, if so, what is it? For example, what moral principles come into play? (integrity, honesty, trustworthiness, impartiality, equity, and exemplary personal character)

Who is being harmed in this situation?

What should be done?

Scenario Four

Julie is a doctoral student in a criminal justice program. Her doctoral dissertation is a study of court-ordered parenting classes. She is trying to determine what type of parenting class intervention has the greater success rate for decreasing occurrence of child abuse. Julie has been working on her dissertation on and off for the past five years. Her school has informed her that she has one year to complete her work or she will not be allowed to continue. Julie has been taking so long trying to complete the requirements due to her personal time commitments. Julie is a single mom of two children, ages twelve and fourteen. She has been working three part-time jobs for the past four years. Julie has been having problems gathering the data needed for her dissertation due to time constraints. She has about 75 percent of her data gathered but needs to have surveys completed from four more parenting groups in order for her to be able to complete the data analysis as proposed. Once that data is in she will still need to conduct the data analysis and finish the chapters in the dissertation. Feeling cornered, Julie decides to fabricate the data on the surveys she needs. She then runs the analysis, completes the dissertation and graduates. Based on her data analysis, one of the parenting programs proves to have positive results. Based on the results of her dissertation, several State Child Protective Services decide to use that program in the future and receive funding from the state in order to provide the program.

Is there an ethical dilemma and, if so, what is it? For example, what moral principles come into play? (integrity, honesty, trustworthiness, impartiality, equity, and exemplary personal character)

If the university were to discover that the data was falsified and the final analysis inaccurate, should there be a penalty imposed on Julie?

What should be done in reference to the state funding a particular parenting program based on the dissertation results? Do you think the university is obligated to inform the state funding source of the situation?

If you were Julie, and faced with a similar situation, what would you have done?

Ethics and the Public's Perception

Criminal justice professionals act under a great deal of public scrutiny, some occupations more so than others, such as policing. Media coverage of unethical police practices has caused a great deal of controversy and has often created heated discussion over how best to reign in the police. This is nothing new, although many of today's college students associate negative press with the Rodney King incident. Most of the parents of today's college students could recount stories of police and public confrontations from the 1960s and the grandparents could probably tell of other such negative incidents happening when they were young. Although it could probably be shown that unethical police behavior has taken place over the past several decades, even centuries, the difference with today's world is the media coverage of such events. Technology enables the public to be kept up-to-date on events around the world. Events are often covered live on television as they are taking place as well as through computer networking. The public often forms its view of police activities from this media coverage. This is not to say that media exposure of unethical police behavior should not take place. What does have to be taken into consideration is that, to a great degree, people form their perception of the police based on what they see and hear about a particular incident.

This is not just true of policing, although that is one occupational field within criminal justice that does receive a great deal of media attention. The formation of the public's perception of all criminal justice services comes largely from what they hear, read, and see as presented by the media. Actions taken by elected officials, such as judges, prosecutors, and sheriffs, also draw the attention of the media as do jail and prison operations. Negative press about a particular situation has a way of affecting perceptions of entire professions, departments, or agencies.

It is important for you to recognize that when you enter a criminal justice profession, your actions and behaviors are likely to be under public scrutiny. Whether you feel this is just or right is not relevant to the discussion. It is a reality that what you do both on and off the job will likely be subject to media attention. The advancements in technology have made real-time coverage of events much more possible than even a decade ago. The unfortunate reality is that stories that sell are usually stories that entail unethical behavior on the part of government employees or elected officials. To be in a government position automatically brings with it public attention and, hence, media coverage of activities and events.

Ethical Challenges to Be Faced

Due to the very nature of the work in criminal justice, many professionals in these occupations will be faced with situations where they have to make a choice based on professional and/or personal ethics. Many criminal justice professionals perform their job responsibilities independently. They are frequently in situations that present opportunities for unethical and even illegal behavior. Choices that they make can have long-lasting effects on their careers as well as the image and reputation of a division, agency, department, or even an entire occupational sector. As mentioned in the previous section, the public often forms its opinion of an entire criminal justice occupation based on the unethical actions of one individual or a small group of individuals. When it comes to passing judgment on the actions of government employees, it appears that, from the public's perspective, one bad apple might spoil the whole batch.

Many police officers are faced with important ethical decisions on a regular basis. They are frequently in situations where people may offer them money or services in return for special treatment, such as not writing a parking or traffic ticket. In the beginning of this chapter we used the words *equity* and *impartiality* to define ethical behavior in context of our discussion. If the officer makes the decision to treat citizens differently based on how much he can personally gain from the situation, then he is not treating all citizens with

equity and impartiality. Everyone he is sworn to serve is not getting the same treatment. Patrol officers are frequently the first people on the scene of a burglary. Items not taken by the thief may be readily available for the taking by those called to the scene. Again, the choice the officer makes based on personal and professional ethical standards can have a long-lasting impact. Patrol officers and specialized units involved in enforcing laws against gambling, prostitution, and drugs are also presented with situations that call for ethical decisions. In fact, in almost every facet of an officer's job she can be faced with situations that require ethical decisions.

The same is true of many of the other occupations in criminal justice. For example, correctional officers working in jails and prisons may be offered bribes by inmates or the inmates' families in return for special goods or services. Probation and parole officers may be offered money, goods, or services to overlook an infraction that could jeopardize the client's freedom. Public defenders may also be offered bribes to provide special services, alter court documents, disregard witness statements, or any one of countless unethical and illegal activities.

It is not hard to imagine the various situations criminal justice professionals encounter that require a decision based on personal and professional ethical standards, four of which have been illustrated in this chapter. What is important is that you think through these possibilities ahead of time, reflect on how you think you would handle the situation, participate in class discussions in which alternative actions are proposed, and critically examine what the consequences of various actions are likely to be. It is through this type of reflective, interactive approach that you may be able to more clearly define for yourself where you stand on ethical issues and how this relates to your chosen profession. It is better to be prepared for the possible choices to be made than to make rash decisions at the time of the event that you are likely to regret later.

Although you can engage in various educational experiences, reflective thinking, and planned decision making pertaining to ethical choices, there are still likely to be situations on the job that are difficult to handle. For example, you may be partnered with someone else who makes unethical decisions. Failure to report such actions can lead to determinations of guilt by association and sometimes criminal charges. Knowing that another criminal justice professional has acted unethically and not doing something is likely to be considered unethical behavior as well. Going to your supervisor would be the first recommendation, but if that does not appear to be a positive course to follow then seeking other agency or department personnel who can assist would be the next step. Many departments and agencies have employee assistance programs. This may be another possible way of handling the situation. In any case, it is important to recognize that knowing about unethical behavior and failing to act on that knowledge can be cause for disciplinary action, termination, or even criminal conviction. Always keep in mind the phrase, "guilt by association." Whether it is through formal channels, such as those just mentioned, or informal channels such as ostracizing an individual, failure to promote or transfer, or any one of a number of other repercussions, the individual is likely to pay the cost of associating with those who act unethically.

Personal Experience

Although the code of ethics was made available when I was hired as a state probation and parole officer, to this day I cannot remember what it stated. Not much attention was paid to the significance of the code during our initial training period or during our required annual training sessions or during our day-to-day delivery of services.

There were times, however, when I had ethical concerns about what happened on the job because of my personal moral principles and beliefs. For example, a major concern I had was in the difference in sentences given to offenders based on factors that had little or nothing to do with the offense. There were also many times when I felt the criminal justice system should be doing more for preventing criminal acts as well as providing services that could prove beneficial to offenders in such areas as education, employment, and substance abuse. There were times when I felt torn between what my job duties and responsibilities were and what I personally felt would be in the public's and client's best interest. I was also concerned that, if I stepped out of the prescribed job description, I would be in violation of some regulation, policy, or procedure.

Did a code of ethics guide my actions as a probation and parole officer? Probably, but it is hard to really discern because, as mentioned before, I don't even remember the code. What, then, did guide my behavior? In my particular situation, I know that my actions were guided more by my own personal principles, based on my background and upbringing, than a professional code. On reflection, I feel more attention should be given to the professional code of ethics on an ongoing basis for all employees. If there are to be expectations of behavioral conduct, then it is only fair that the employees be informed of the expectations, educated on the consequences for infractions, and their ethical compliance encouraged through agency training and open discussions.

Activity 9.1   Principles of Behavior

Make a list of all the basic principles of behavior you were taught as a child. After each principle, note in what context you learned this principle such as from parents, school staff, peers, church, and any others that may apply.

_____
_____
_____
_____
_____
_____
_____
_____
_____
_____
_____
_____
_____
_____
_____
_____
_____
_____
_____
_____
_____
_____
_____
_____
_____
_____

Activity 9.2   Code of Ethics and Principles

Using textbooks, Web sites, or trade journals, locate a code of ethics for the career track you chose in Chapter 3. Compare the list that you developed in Activity 9.1 to the code and write down all of the principles that match the expectations listed in the code. Next, make a list of all the behavioral expectations in the code that you feel may be a challenge to fulfill, with a brief explanation as to why.

_____

_____

_____

_____

_____

_____

_____

_____

_____

_____

_____

_____

_____

_____

_____

_____

_____

_____

_____

_____

_____

_____

_____

_____

_____

_____

10
After Graduation: What Then?

The material and activities in the previous chapters were provided to assist you in making the transition from being a student to entering your future career in criminal justice. As should be apparent by now, personal and honest reflection is a main ingredient needed to successfully make this transition. Although time intensive, you will likely find that reflection is time well spent to develop positive outcomes, for example, satisfaction with your career choice and good job performance. Knowing who you are as a person, recognizing your strengths and weaknesses, and learning what it takes to make educated decisions about career choices is all part of making the transition from student to criminal justice professional. If you are continuing your education, you will most likely enter the program with a career goal in mind. Again, this goal should be the product of thoughtful reflection and educated decision making.

Careers are major life choices. Everything you do prior to graduation will contribute to the probability of not only your employability but finding a good fit between personal goals and career duties and responsibilities. You should view your involvement in college education not just as a means to learn something but also as a time during which you can develop your skills in communication and critical thinking as well as your personal work habits, including punctuality, consistency in professional work product, time management, and task organization. It is also during your college years that you are presented with many opportunities for developing networks and establishing your reputation in the profession. The main point is that everything that you do during your college years should build toward a positive outcome. Your future economic stability, job security, and career growth depend on these preliminary stages.

How do you find a good fit between who you are as a person, your career choice, and the duties and re-

sponsibilities that come with that choice? A positive step in that direction would be integrating the material covered in this book and individualizing it by completing the activities that make it personally relevant. Figure 10.1 provides a graphic representation of the integration of the concepts presented so you can more clearly understand what needs to be taken into consideration in finding your fit. What happens if the fit cannot be found? This chapter provides a discussion of alternative career choices related to criminal justice. How do you expand your career once you get a job in criminal justice? This chapter provides suggestions on how to keep fresh, keep your interest involved, and keep your opportunities open. What can happen when you are promoted from a line service job to an administrative position? This chapter provides information to help you understand what to expect. Finally, the chapter concludes with an overview of what you should be able to accomplish by completing the readings and activities in this book.

Integration of Book Material

As should be evident by now, the concepts presented in previous chapters were designed to provide you with an integrated perspective on the transition from college to career. Integrating material and ideas from one chapter to the next should provide you with the tools necessary to make informed decisions about your future in criminal justice. After completing all of the activities in the previous chapters, it is now crucial that you recognize the relevance of the sum of all the individual parts. Figure 10.1 is provided to illustrate the integration of the book concepts.

In Chapter 1, I described how I thought being a police officer was my dream career, but soon found out differently. Although I had the education needed for the

CRIMINAL JUSTICE MAJOR	+	Core and General Education Requirements	+	Goals, Interests, Values, Strengths, & Weaknesses	+	Extracurricular Involvement	+	Identification of & Information about Preferred Career Track	=	BACHELOR DEGREE AND MARKETABILITY

Combined with

Awareness of the Influence of Politics	+	Understanding of the Importance of Networking	+	Awareness of Personal Ethics & Professional Codes	+	Awareness of Career Related Challenges	=	JOB "FIT"

Which Can Lead to

Increased Job Satisfaction
Increased Job Performance
Decreased Job Turnover

FIGURE 10.1

position, I had really not thought through how the duties and responsibilities of the job fit who I was as a person. I had developed my own expectations of what the job would be like based mainly on fictional information gleaned through television shows. I had not taken the time to educate myself on what I could realistically expect and I did not understand the significance of networking, politics, and various challenges in this line of work. I was marketable through my education and I had chosen a career track, but I had not carefully thought through how my personal goals, interests, and values fit the job. In other words, I had not integrated valuable information into the choices I made. The consequence was poor job satisfaction and turnover. Activity 10.1 is provided to assist you in gaining a better understanding of the integration of the concepts and information provided in this book, something that would have assisted me a great deal.

Alternative Career Choices

Even with the best efforts at gaining information, personal reflection, and planning, there are times when things, for a variety of reasons, don't turn out the way one expects. I have always been a strong believer in the high value of a criminal justice degree. This is a degree that can be used to gain employment either directly within the criminal justice system, as with policing and probation work, or indirectly with a variety of employment opportunities in other occupational service fields.

Career opportunities are numerous, including employment possibilities in a variety of disciplines such as education, counseling, work development, health services, program evaluation, research, and government planning and management. Of course, employment in these fields will depend, to a great extent, on the student's educational background and previous experience. Therefore, it is highly recommended that you seriously consider what classes you are going to take to fulfill your elective requirements. For example, if you are interested in counseling juvenile delinquents, then you should take courses in other disciplines such as child and adolescent development, personality testing, and counseling techniques for your electives. These courses can usually be found in the psychology, education, or counseling divisions. Even if you are fairly confident that you will be content with a chosen profession directly related to criminal justice, it is in your best interest to take some of your electives in some area that builds on your criminal justice degree rather than take whatever general elective credits fit into your schedule, regardless of future benefit.

Another way that you can help build your credentials for future employment is through internship placements, a topic discussed in detail in Chapter 4. For example, if you are interested in program planning and evaluation, an internship with a government planning office would be appropriate. As well as improving your marketability, you would be developing valuable networks.

Yet another way in which you can augment your criminal justice degree and widen your career opportunities is through workshops or training provided by local agencies or associations. You can find out about training offered through local agencies by calling those agencies and asking about upcoming events. Some agency training will be open to nonemployees while some will not. It is also to your benefit to attend workshops and training for networking purposes, a topic discussed in detail in Chapter 8. Attending these events will give you an opportunity to meet professionals in a variety of fields as well as gaining insights about various jobs.

There are two points to be made: (1) it is better to have a couple of alternative career choices in mind and prepare for these alternatives by taking elective courses or even a minor in these areas, and (2) even if your anticipated career falls short of expectations, the degree is still a good, solid degree that can open many doors in other related fields. You need to recognize that, if you find yourself in a job that does not fit, you do not have to throw out the whole degree. You may just need to explore related options to find what works best for you. Life is too short to stay in a job that just does not fit. The appendix at the end of this book provides a list of possible careers using a criminal justice degree. Although it represents only a partial list of possibilities, it should be enough to illustrate that there are many choices available.

Expanding Career Potential

After you are employed in your career track for a few years, you may find that you either want to or are required to expand your duties and responsibilities with your current employer. Promotions or advancements within career tracks often require a change in job responsibilities and duties. In order to better prepare for these changes it is to your benefit to take part in related workshops, training, and conferences. Taking the initiative to grow *with* the job can put you in a better position for promotions. For example, if a probation officer wants to advance into a supervisory position, it would be to her benefit to attend workshops or training that promotes skills necessary for the position such as leadership, personnel management, and budgeting. Competition for administrative positions can often be high, so it is to your benefit to find ways in which you can market yourself when an opening is available. Another way in which you can better prepare yourself for promotions is to volunteer for extra assignments while in your current position. This shows upper manage-

ment that you are willing to put in the extra effort to improve your knowledge, skills, and abilities.

As was discussed in detail in Chapter 8, networking can be a valuable tool in your pursuit of career advancement. In the real world, there are likely to be government positions that are filled based on who you know. Of course, most of us would agree that what you know should be the criterion for job placement. Recognizing what happens in the real world can be to your advantage and you can combine what you know with who you know to put yourself in the best possible position to get the advancement you desire. Networking as a means of marketing yourself is to be expected.

Historically, in many government agencies, there has been a tendency to promote strictly based on seniority. If you are promoted without preparation for the new responsibilities and duties, you may find yourself in a difficult position that can impact your personal job satisfaction and performance as well as impacting the overall operations of the entire unit. Even though a promotion may appear to be a positive move based on increased pay and/or prestige, being in a position where you feel you cannot meet the expectations is usually not a comfortable feeling. One way to cope with such a situation is to seek the training and education needed for the position. Another way is to ask to shadow someone currently fulfilling similar responsibilities and learn through observation. The problem with this approach is that some of those people may not be good role models to follow due to their personal lack of knowledge, skills, and abilities.

Promotion is generally seen as a positive move, and can be just that. It may not only provide increases in income and be a stepping stone for future advancement, but it can also add the challenge many need to keep the job interesting. In a perfect world everyone receiving a promotion would have the requisite knowledge, skills, and abilities to best meet the expectations of new job responsibilities and duties. In the real world, the responsibility for preparedness probably rests more so on the individual than it does on the employer. Recognizing this reality, you should do everything within your ability to prepare for future opportunities and to get up to speed quickly if you are promoted to a position without adequate preparation.

Staying Fresh

There may be times when, although you are working in a job that you are comfortable with, you just don't feel as energized, challenged, or interested in your work as you did when you first started. This is probably a natural response to doing more or less the same thing, day in and day out. Although comfortable in the position, meaning that you aren't inclined to seek a new job or apply for advancement, there may be a feeling of boredom and lack of contentment. There are activities that can help you stay fresh and interested in your work.

Criminal justice is a fascinating discipline with often rapid and dramatic developments based on factors such as technological advancements, political changes, shifts in public opinion, and increased diversity. After all my years of involvement with criminal justice, I continue to view it as a challenging and fascinating discipline. There is something happening in criminal justice every day on a local, state, national, and international level.

One way to stay fresh and interested is to know what is happening around you. Keeping current through reading or watching the news everyday is one way to do this. Reading articles in trade journals is another way. You can subscribe to them or access the material through local libraries or on the Web. Your employer may subscribe to some of these journals as well.

Another way to stay up-to-date is to attend training and workshops provided by your employer or through another agency. Just getting your name on the mailing list for announcements through training institutes will assist in keeping you abreast of your opportunities. Employers are sometimes willing to pay enrollment fees if you can show that the information to be provided will, in some way, relate to your work.

Yet another avenue in which you can stay on top of some of the latest developments in criminal justice is to attend professional conferences. In Chapter 4, participation in these events was encouraged in order to make yourself marketable. Once in a job, participation can help keep you informed as well as to provide you with an opportunity to network with other professionals in the field. Again, getting on the mailing list for notification of upcoming conference dates is the first step to opening the door to more involvement in your field of interest. The two main professional organizations specific to criminal justice are the Academy of Criminal Justice Sciences and the American Society of Criminology. There are also conferences held by regional criminal justice associations.

Taking college courses is yet another way to learn something new as well as to build your academic cre-

dentials for future career advancements or changes. With the rapid changes occurring in the field of criminal justice often comes a need for special topics courses designed to keep students abreast of recent developments. For example, technological advancements in forensic science have changed investigative techniques dramatically. Policy changes based on recent legal decisions call for updated education that is often provided through special topics courses. Taking additional college courses after graduation is often a very different experience than prior to having gained work experience and can give you a sense of challenge, while at the same time giving you an opportunity to improve your credentials for the future.

Volunteering for special projects within your current employment is yet another way to keep your interest level up and to grow through new experiences. For example, there may be an opportunity to participate with the planning and research team or department of your agency. Or you may have a chance to help develop a grant proposal for additional funding needed to provide a new program such as parenting classes for incarcerated juvenile delinquents. In criminal justice, the needs for services are varied and numerous. Usually, all that is required is an interest and a commitment on the part of someone to provide a service to meet the need. By volunteering for such projects you are not only helping to fulfill this need but you are giving yourself an opportunity to stay challenged and to learn something that could open doors for you in the future.

Yet another way to keep interested and challenged in your current profession is to join a committee or advisory group that addresses criminal justice issues in which you are interested. There are many such opportunities available in most communities, and they offer a broad range of involvement in widely diverse areas. For example, the local police department may have a crime prevention task force, the mayor's office may have an advisory board for community development, the local jail may have a committee whose responsibility is to explore local alternative sentencing options, and the prosecutor's office may have a victims' advocacy panel. How do you get involved in such activities? Sometimes it is as simple as making a phone call and volunteering. It may require a more formal process entailing submitting a current résumé or meeting with county or city commissioners and getting a formal appointment. Your ability to become involved in community advisory boards, panels, committees, or activist groups will most likely depend on your level of commitment to such a goal.

Along these lines, you may find that, with your increased involvement in projects and services as well as continued learning through training, workshops, conferences, and course involvement, you want to petition to revise your job description. Your employer is likely to find your willingness to change your job description to more accurately reflect your duties and responsibilities a definite asset, and that can improve your job performance ratings and job security. However, you may find yourself in a situation in which your employer discourages you from becoming involved in any activities outside of your current job description. In this case you will have to decide whether you will be content to stay where you are or consider other opportunities in your area of interest.

There are many ways in which you can keep your interest level up in what you are currently doing and find new challenges. The individual has the responsibility for taking the initiative to be involved. The rewards are often worth the effort.

Second Careers

Second careers are different from changing careers. A second career is most likely to come about after you have retired from a first career. For example, police officers who complete twenty-five years of service can retire at the age of forty-seven, and they are still young enough to start another career. Some people will be able to move into a second career as a result of their job experiences. In this case, they are most likely to enter a second career in the same general field they worked in during their first career.

Others may decide that they want a second career that, although utilizing their prior experiences, will lead them in a different direction. For example, someone may retire out of corrections work, having completed twenty or more years as a case manager, and decide that he wants to become a school teacher and work with troubled youth. This career change may require continued education and/or licensing. In this case, it is highly recommended that, before reaching retirement age, the person gather information about requirements for the second career option and start working to complete these a few years before retiring. This may require enrolling as an undergraduate or graduate student in a particular program. For many of us, it is financially difficult to stop working while

we attend school, especially after we have increased our financial obligations through the years. Therefore, taking a few classes each year toward a new degree or working toward a particular licensing requirement over time may be the best solution.

Changing to a second career with different duties, responsibilities, and, perhaps, degree requirements will basically require you to start again with the activities provided throughout this book. Once again, it goes back to making informed decisions and, in order to do so, you will have to educate yourself on your chosen career option just as if this was your first career.

The number and variety of career options available for graduates with a criminal justice degree are limited only by the level of interest and motivation of the person. Whether it be changes of job duties and responsibilities, mid-career changes to other jobs within the criminal justice field or related jobs, promotions, or second careers, the opportunities are numerous.

Conclusion

Careers in criminal justice can be personally rewarding and fulfilling. The sense of pride you get in being able to help another human being, in even the smallest way, is a feeling that can keep you energized to work in an occupation that is often stressful, dangerous, and frustrating. Education is one step you can take to prepare for a career. But being prepared also requires being in touch with personal goals, interest, values, strengths, and weaknesses, in other words, knowing who you are as a person. Being prepared also requires you to educate yourself on the realities and challenges of the job in order to know what to expect and how you, personally, fit your chosen criminal justice career track.

The activities in this book were provided to encourage you to think outside the box, and there was a heavy emphasis on reflection. It is through reflection that you will be able to gain a better understanding of how you fit your chosen career. It is important to always remember that finding your fit requires awareness not only of what you bring to the job but also what the job brings to you. It is through awareness of the influence of politics, networking, and ethics, as well as the relevance of developed knowledge, skills, and abilities, that you will be able to find the best fit in career choice.

Activity 10.1   Putting It All Together Once More

Using small index cards, outline key points you personally learned from the information and activities in each chapter. For example, from Chapter 1 you would make a card that lists your values, another card that lists your strengths, and so on. From Chapter 6 you would use a card to outline what you learned from the test or survey you took through the career placement office. From Chapter 7 you would outline how you see politics impacting your particular career choice, and from Chapter 8 you would use a card to outline the network for your chosen career. The important thing to remember is that you are using these cards to outline how the information can be applied to you, individually. After you have created these cards, your next step is to place them on a large poster-board. Don't glue them on at first because you will likely see that you will want to arrange the cards in an order that integrates the information in a way that makes sense to you. There is no need to follow any structured format for creating your poster. The purpose of this assignment is to have you picture how the pieces of information you have learned can be integrated to give you direction for the future, and to encourage you to continue the reflection process.

Appendix

Corrections

Jail Administrator
Warden/Superintendent
Business Manager
Line Correctional Officer
Inmate Classification
Prison Industries Superintendent
Child Care Staff
Academic
Psychologist
Institution Parole Officer
Casework Supervisor
Vocational Instructor
Classification Officer
Social Worker
Media Representative
Legal Representative
Probation/Parole Officer
Custodial Officer

Enforcement

Patrol Officer
Investigation Officer
Traffic officer
Sheriff
Fish and Game Warden
Juvenile Officer
Dispatcher
Community Relations Officer
Fire Marshal
Special Agent (FBI, IRS, DEA, ATF)
Secret Service

Military Intelligence
Military Police
Security Officers
Retail Loss Prevention
Border Patrol Agents
Private Investigations
U.S. Marshal

Courts

Prosecuting Attorney
Defense Attorney
Paralegal/Legal Aid Counselor
Judge
Court Administrator
Bailiff
Court Clerk
Social Worker
Translator
Court Reporter
Psychological Evaluator
Intake Worker

Other Related Occupations

Criminal Justice Researcher
Government Planner
Journalist
Insurance Fraud Investigator
Postal Inspector
Forensic Science
Community Service Programs
Child Protective Services